MW00619769

Grace House Publishing
USA
www.gracehousepublishing.com
Information on this title at www.gracehousepublishing.com/10022015

This publication is in copyright. Subject to statutory exception and to the provision of relevant licensing agreements, no reproduction of any part may take place without the written permission of its author, Olivia M. McDonald.

2nd Edition, Copyright 2015
Printed in the United States of America
Library of Congress Cataloguing in Publication Data

ACKNOWLEDGING GOD IN THE DECISIONS OF *STATE: A Treatise on Biblical Statesmanship* *authored by Olivia M. McDonald*
ISBN-13: 978-0-9835652-0-8 (E-book)
ISBN-10: 0-9835652-0-1 (E-book)
ISBN-10: 0-9835652-3-6 (Paper)
ISBN-13: 978-0-9835652-3-9 (Paper)
ISBN-10: 0983565252 (Hardcover)
ISBN-13: 978-0-9835652-5-3(Hardcover)

1. God 2.Public Policy Analysis   3.Decision Making   4.Church and State Relations
5. Biblical Statesmanship
I. McDonald, Olivia M.   1954-

Grace House Publishing has no responsibility for the persistence or accuracy of URLs for external or third-part Internet Web sites referred to in this publication and does not guarantee than any content on such websites is, or will remain, accurate or appropriate.

To

YESHUA

Sovereign of the Universe

Creator of the Heavens and the Earth,

Who Redeems and Counsels

&

Who Gives to Me Memories of

Rufus L. & Nona C. Hardeman,
My Wonderful Parents

Thank You!

CONTENTS

Preface

PART ONE: *Challenges*

PART TWO: *Opportunities*

LIST of TABLES & FIGURES

*P*REFACE

"The Bible is government of the people, by the people, and for the people." -
--John Wycliffe, Morningstar of the Reformation

*W*hen a close colleague and I last spoke, she said that there were far too many
competing voices for someone to really know what was true about religion---much less
knowledge of Jesus Christ She found it difficult to see what any discussion about God
or the Holy Bible had to offer of tangible value to an individual or society at-large. I
took that conversation to heart and wrote the book you now hold.

To be clear, right from the offset:

To govern is to execute law. To govern well is to execute just law, law derived from the
written Word of God, the Holy Bible. To quote John Wycliffe, 'The Holy Bible is
government of the people, by the people, and for the people.'[1] I am in agreement with
Wycliffe's statement primarily because I believe that it is only within the parameters of
God's law that a nation can operate in freedom, affording liberty to exercise the moral
clarity required to make righteous decisions, and thus rendering conditions that permit
citizenry to thrive. Quite simply put, my premise is this: The status of nations--the
degree to which governing bodies successfully navigate the challenges that confront their
respective jurisdictions-- is a direct by-product of adherence to and the execution of
God's law by those who govern, thus rightly Acknowledging God in the Decisions of
State.

Acknowledging God in Decisions of State exists as a remedy to the very common
confusion concerning the appropriate role of Christian belief in the process of
governance. The goal here is to make sense of what sounds like disharmonious rhetoric,
describing that which would have little to no value to those outside the faith.

Concerning the audience for this work, know that I am writing to all of those who are
like my dear friend, folks possessing keen intellect yet lacking the divine spark of
understanding that knowledge of the Holy One of Israel grants. And, to my Christian

colleagues, this book is for you, too! This book is for the "people" who C.S. Lewis once described in the following passage from *Mere Christianity*,

> ...By the Church they ought to mean the whole body of practicing Christians. And when they say that the Church should give us a lead, they ought to mean that some Christians--- those who happen to have the right talents---should be economists and statesmen, and that all economists and statesmen should be Christians, and their whole efforts of politics and economics should be directed to putting "Do as you would be done by" into action. If that happened, and if we others were really ready to take it, then we should find the Christian solution for our own social problems pretty quickly.[2]

This book holds important correspondence for all who are called to be "Salt" and "Light" in this world. *Why?* Well, the reason is simple. There is a problem afoot. The problem is that no good can emanate from mixed signals or garbled speech from those charged with sharing the gospel of Jesus Christ. In an age plagued with terrorist threat, a difference between Egypt and Goshen ought to be easily recognizable. Unfortunately, traditional social indicators suggest distinction is not the case. For some reason it is as if with all our good intentions, we who adhere to the Judeo-Christian tradition have assembled a litany of competing sounds, not sung in divine harmony, sounds that do not herald a better alternative in this life, but instead sounds that have inadvertently distracted from the most important voice of all---that of God.

I once heard a Washington D.C. minister best put the situation this way,

"In a universe that was spoken into existence, God cannot afford to lose His voice!" [3]

By *Acknowledging God in the Decisions of State*, I am not suggesting that religion should be used as a political ploy to win elections.[4] Nor, am I saying that violations of conscience should be tolerated as a consequence of state actions. What I am saying is that among those that profess to know Christ Jesus, individuals who purport to believe in and ascribe to the written Word of God, the Holy Bible, those God-Fearing people are to be salt and light wherever God has placed them, and that includes in positions of governance.

This book gives insight into the current obstacles to good governance encountered in the United States, offering lessons applicable to all nations. And, by good governance, I am referring to the presence of governmental decision-making, consistent with the written Word of God, the Holy Bible. Obedience to God's Word honors and glorifies God.

This book also discusses opportunities that may emerge to improve government decision making. Indeed, the point is made that in order to reduce the frequency with which policy decisions miss the mark, right relationship with God must be established, a relationship that has as a byproduct the moral clarity required of God-fearing individuals who He has placed in positions of governance. This is in recognition of the fact that:

---Moral clarity maximizes the survivability of populations; and,

---Moral clarity must not be limited only to persons in prominent positions of governance. Indeed, in the United States, a Constitutional Republic, the expectation at time of inception was that moral clarity would exist in order for the people to be self-governing, meaning self-controlled, a character trait which is the fruit of the Spirit of God.[5]

To the degree that "self-control" is absent among the leaders and the populace, demands increase for government intervention. This is in large part because the problems confronting the society, problems that stem from moral breakdown, yield challenges perceived as overwhelming for the individual. Further, to the degree that relationship with God becomes nonexistent, one may expect many to seek help from other quarters beyond family, as moral breakdown has dealt a severe blow to that God-given institution. And, when, for the same or related reasons, help may not be forthcoming, many will seek help from the State.

The absence of reliance upon God means complete reliance upon man and manmade institutional arrangements that have morphed into configurations incompatible with God's design. To the degree that individuals rely upon the systems of man, the greater the degree to which those very systems will redefine what is problematic for that individual. In regimes where the State defines the bulk of existence, the definition replacement is total. That is in essence the nature of "totalitarian" regimes. In such governmental settings, people exist for the State. The State does not exist for the people. The progression toward totalitarianism derives from ever increasing dependency upon the State, yielding enslavement under the guise of provision and protection.

A sort of *"policy genealogy"* emerges where one policy begets another policy which in turn begets yet another policy.

God-honoring character traits, what the Holy Bible refers to as the fruits of the Spirit, when present among citizenry and its leadership, often diminishes the need for reliance upon government intervention. Such traits liberate the individual to pursue "happiness," meaning the pursuit of progress as reflects fulfillment of all that God has endowed.

Avoidance of enslavement begins with the thought processes associated with knowing who one is in relation to God; and, knowing what is of value given God's perspective. Because each human being is made in the image of God, great expanse exists, tremendous potential, free for us to tap into without bounds. Martyrs have known such freedom, a realization of God that is more undeniable than the flames of torture experienced. A society made up of people in possession of that kind of understanding will not become easily susceptible to self-imposed enslavement.

Man, nevertheless, is fallen. Institutions and abominable acts can and have emerged that are extensions of that fallen nature: institutions such as slavery, and atrocities such as genocide, the Holocaust.

---Such has occurred by the hands of some who proclaimed to be followers of the God of the Holy Bible, and with others who served as accomplices by virtue of their decisive silence.

---Such silence is damnable.

God's Providence must never again be offered as an excuse for tolerating wrong, as it once was argued in response to opponents of the blight of Slavery experienced in the United States; and, also as tolerance for the outrageous devastation experienced by Jews during the Holocaust. This is also the reason why the problem of replacement theology is so horrendous. Replacement theology twists focus away from moral responsibility to that of justifiable tolerance for the intolerable anywhere on earth, but especially with regard to Israel. Definitions that are inconsistent with God's perspective are deadly.

Failure to acknowledge God in the decisions of state puts at jeopardy the sovereignty of the United States and the well-being of the rest of the nations around the world. Because the United States and Israel are nations founded on the Bible, we have those fundamental biblical principles at the core of our system of governance. We the people are people of the Book! The sovereignty of the United States and the well-being of the rest of the nations of the world become jeopardized when our leaders fail to acknowledge God of the Bible in the decisions of state because:

> ➢ God establishes nations in an effort to get our attention[6];

> ➢ Nations are judged in our life time, not in eternity;

> ➢ Our nation was founded on biblical principles and because of that fact God's name is at stake;

> ➢ Only where God is acknowledged is there Liberty for the individual;

> ➢ Since God of the Bible is the only one who authors life and hope, biblically-informed decision-making is required to maintain and expand liberty in the world;

> ➢ The most significant threat to God-Given Liberty is the bondage that finds justification because of the lack of self control and the presence of addictive behavior;

> ➢ Among the nations, God has made certain assurances about Israel. We who align ourselves with God must align ourselves with Israel;

> ➢ The Constitutional Republic form of governance as found in the United States assumes prerequisite character traits that are to be shared by government decision-makers;

> ➢ The operational structure of governance in the United States is conditioned upon slow change; and, as a consequence, any errors in reasoning may steadily get worse, building upon faulty decisions, not easily reverted;

> ➢ Gaps in information are not shored up because God has operationally structured a need for Himself in the life of individuals and nations;

> ➢ God renders futile the judgment of those that are distanced from Him; and,

> ➢ Ultimately, a relation exists between belief system (faith) and the perception of risk. The absence of faith is terror, one of the first curses experienced as a result of prodigal status as listed in the book of Leviticus, a result of persistent distance from God.

"RETURN TO ME," SAYS THE LORD

By *Acknowledging God in the Decisions of State*, I am referring to the need to make a conscious decision to seek a biblical understanding of the issues confronting our individual and collective life. It is because God goes ignored that activity resulting in goal accomplishment becomes difficult. This is due in part because any success must rely heavily upon communication. What one attempts to communicate, if not graced by God, results in distorted messages, sounding much like a car radio dial stuck between two, unintelligible, stations.

Relying on the biblical account, we know that the first borders between human beings on this earth were words. That fact is well worth remembering these days. From Genesis, the earliest part of history, humanity was engaged in the first major recorded public works project. The project was the construction of the Tower of Babel.[7] This tower project resulted in futility because the project itself went into operation counter the instructions God had given humanity. As passages in Genesis remind us, God said to be fruitful and multiply, and to subdue the earth. Instead, in direct violation of that command and under the governmental leadership of Nimrod, the decision of state was to build the Tower. I realize that "Towers" conjure up many emotions these days since 9/11 in the United States, but this Tower itself was to be located in Babylon and the rationale given for pursuing the project was "so that the people might make a name for themselves." The populace went to work, united in this initiative---that is to say that at least no opposition was galvanized enough to make it into recorded public record about this project. Political consensus was that the Tower Project was a good idea. God, however, apparently was not asked if he had changed His mind about what He had commanded. In response to the population's failure to acknowledge Him, God scrambled the language and thus aborted all collaborative activity for a time while folks sought out those who could understand each other, speaking the same language.

Before God took it upon Himself to scramble communication, He had all of humanity speaking one language. Language was a gift from Him so that human beings could first communicate with God. Communication made marriage possible. Correspondingly there would be fruitful multiplication and the needed communication required for subduing the earth. In other words, members of humanity could talk to each other. Imagine! There was but one language that everybody spoke. That meant unity of conceptualization, accurate understanding of the messages conveyed. But, because misguided decisions were made with idolatrous intent, God rendered the language and its outworking futile.

This pattern of right relationship with God to the point of acknowledgment, yielding right communication with the rest of humanity is non-trivial. Since action should be explanation driven [otherwise action would be simply mania], I posit that only one of two possible scenarios in varying configurations is likely to occur as a consequence of senseless, non-recognition of God: either (1) flawed explanation yielding flawed action---flawed in the since of having either partial elements of truth , incomplete, held with apparent correctness of form, yet possessing significant gaps in understanding thus compromising our ability to arrive at appropriate solutions to problems; or, (2) flawed action results because the correct explanation offered may exist in such a vacuum as to prohibit successful implementation. Desired outcomes cannot be achieved because the component parts of implementation suffer fragmentation due to the lack of cohering truth. The outcomes I have described represent opposite ends of a continuum. I graphically depict the above scenarios as a grid consisting of four quadrants: **Correct Explanation/Coherent Implementation; Flawed Explanation/Coherent Implementation; Correct Explanation/Incoherent Implementation; and, Flawed Explanation/Incoherent Implementation.** I prefer to use the word, "flawed" because such a term covers the full spectrum of possible error. Prescriptively my construct takes into consideration error that Francis Bacon warned us about when he introduced us to the scientific method as a way of testing the truthfulness of a claim. Bacon warned us about **idols**---mental constructs of human origin that were obstacles to our seeing Truth. It is the same thinking that recognizes that it is possible to make what some refer to as Type III errors, the error in attempting to solve the wrong problem as a consequence of flawed judgment. The ability to avoid such error is called "discernment." And discernment is a gift that comes from God.

What about God? You might ask. Well, no attempt is made in this book to prove that God exists. However, **highlighted in this book are the adverse consequences of a prodigal nation having been founded on biblical understanding choosing to operate now as if God does not exist.** Maintained in the following pages is the perspective that a promise of great fortune alluringly has seduced the *body politic,* including "the Church," into a "Prodigal Status," the direct result of distancing from God of the Holy Bible.

Some would like to believe "God" to be a myth, a mere subject for Hollywood extravaganza. Who hasn't appreciated the opening monologue of Cecil B. DeMilles, who then presents on cinematic screen the vision of parallel walls of water with the Israelites walking through on dry ground, as a demonstration of God's enormous power. The scene shifts. We see the Israelites safe while the Egyptians, in an attempt to follow on Israeli heels, drown. Jehovah, the Lord God Almighty, sufficient to save, swallows up the enemies of Israel. Now, for those who see such a story as just so much "*hocus pocus,*" you need to be aware of the fact that in 2003 the Egyptian government filed suit against Israel in an attempt to gain reparations for the booty that was taken from Egypt during the Jewish Exodus. Here is the account as presented by Nissan Ratzlav-Katz in posted in the Israel National News.

"According to a translation provided by the Middle East Media Research Institute (MEMRI), the August 9, 2003, edition of the Egyptian weekly al-Ahram al-Arabi includes an interview with Dr. Nabil Hilmi, the Dean of the Law Faculty at al-Zaqazia University. Dr. Hilmi claims that he and a group of Switzerland-based Egyptian patriates, the weekly reports, are preparing a suit to be filed against "all Jews" for property taken from the Egyptians at the time of the Biblical Exodus from Pharaonic Egypt. He estimates the value of the suit to be 'very large, 'at least 1.125 trillion tons of gold (based on a low, but still shari' a-forbidden, 5%annual interest rate)."[8]

With pieces of chariots, etcetera, discovered at the bottom of the sea, Egypt knows that the Exodus as described in the Holy Bible happened and as a consequence they want loss redressed in International Court. *Interesting!*

In the pages that follow concerning primarily the United States, offered is an explanation for voices and the events that having albeit less dramatic appeal, have nonetheless spurned the fruit of seemingly contradictory ideas in the governance of our nation. False concepts fuel much distortion in decision-making these days. So, I begin this book by discussing how two historical events have left many in overwhelming disillusionment, a condition undergirding momentum for government expansion.

My prayer as we begin this exposition is that the God of Abraham, Isaac, and Jacob, the One who is made manifest in Christ Jesus, will guide our thinking as He has done for those before us. I pray recognizing that it is difficult to embark upon a discussion of invisible things in an age where so much credence is paid to the visible. Ironically, when New Age gurus offer combinations of eastern and western concepts, calling that conglomeration "New Spirituality" or some other coinage, very little critique is offered.

This book makes explicit the adverse implications of approaching strategic decision-making in governance that fails to have as its point of departure the ***Acknowledgment of God—the God of Abraham, Isaac, and Jacob***. Then, as a consequence of explaining the patterns that can result, the goal will be to explain how to make biblically sound public policy recommendations in a way that maximizes the likelihood of receptivity even among those who do not share a biblical view of the world. This is accomplished by explaining *(i)* the adverse consequences associated with not acknowledging God---that of futility of effort; *(ii)* the points of access within the policymaking process that lends itself to the introduction of ideas consistent with biblical principles; *(iii)* the development of biblically sound policy narrative; and, *(iv)* means for generating biblically driven evaluation of public policy, its implementation and impact.

Yes, in these pages we consider a biblically informed alternative approach to assessing public policy issues including the tools needed for testing the truthfulness of explanation upon which future action may rest. But, more importantly, we will explore a biblically informed approach to public policy decision making so that God may be honored by our right acknowledgment of God in governance.

Acknowledging God in Decisions of State: A Treatise on Biblical Statesmanship affords an opportunity to discover the alternative of biblically-informed decision making, useful in formulating political discourse, having as the point of departure right acknowledgement of God. With increased understanding through reliance upon the Holy Bible--- the only book that survived the fall of mankind unscathed---we may have a frank discussion of Truth telling especially in times of crisis. We will also discuss the development of public policy narratives that reflect God's perspective rightly resting upon the Holy Bible, His written Word to us, relevant in our present age. Our failure to ACKNOWLEDGE GOD has resulted in Policy Spirals discussed in the next chapter. Let's now turn to Chapter 1, Acknowledging God in Prodigal Nations.

--Olivia M. McDonald

CHAPTER ONE

Acknowledging God in Prodigal Nations

"For although they knew God, they neither glorified him as God nor gave thanks to him, but their thinking became futile and their foolish hearts were darkened. Although they claimed to be wise, they became fools and exchanged the glory of the immortal God for images made to look like mortal man and birds and animals and reptiles."[9]
---Romans 1: 21-23, Holy Bible, NIV

"No people can be bound to acknowledge and adore the Invisible Hand which conducts the affairs of men more than those of the United States. Every step by which they have advanced to the character of an independent nation seems to have been distinguished by some token of Providential agency..." *---George Washington's First Inaugural Address in the City of New York, April 30, 1780*

Governance

  I agree with Stephen McDowell and Mark Beliles, *Liberating the Nations: Biblical Principles of Government, Education, Economics, & Politics.* They state,

> "Every nation operates on the ideas and principles of some religion – be it
> Christian, Muslim, humanism, or whatever. A Christian nation, to remain free
> and prosperous, must operate on Christian principles. Every nation will eat of the
> fruit of the principles on which it operates."[10]

  Consequently, a number of elements should be considered, not the least of which is the strategy for adjustments of focus given the presence of any number of misdirected paths that have become imbedded in our society. The problem of competing problem definitions, non-problematic status of real problems, and the administrative spiraling that has evolved from institutions into policy network configurations will be explored. In addition, the debilitation associated with the challenges against the inerrancy of the Holy Bible will be clearly stated. This problem which stems from eclecticism---the idea that all gods, religions, and philosophies are created equal---has yielded slippage in reasoning and governmental error in our world.

The sovereignty of the United States and the well-being of the rest of the nations of the world become jeopardized when our leaders fail to acknowledge God in the decisions of state because the Constitutional Republic type political structure of governance upon which the U.S. was established assumes prerequisite character traits that are to be shared by government decision-makers. The principle of self-governance requires a self-controlled people, citizenry and their representatives that can make right decisions. Further, it was assumed that God-fearing people would operate in obedience to the law. The law of the land would be based upon the Ten Commandments. Conscience would dictate honorable behavior to be the norm. The constituency must be literate because they must be able to read the word of God to discern good from evil. Also assumed was that the biblically-informed would choose the good over evil. And, finally that self-interest would be seen as being served best by the good.

Another aspect to our political system rests upon an operational structure conditioned upon slow change. In such as structure of governance as that in the U.S., errors in reasoning that progressively get worse build incrementally and are not easily reverted. Career appointments transcend presidential administrations and congressional tenure. The mechanics of getting a piece of legislation passed reduces the likelihood of the introduction of new laws significantly. But beyond the above, there is another aspect to decisions of state that is repeatedly overlooked. Gaps in information exist. The information is required to actually make right decisions may not readily available. In an environment where there is much data, there is very little usable information needed to have success in decision making. God has operationally structured a need for Himself in the lives of individuals and nations. And, coupled with the assessment challenges embedded in our system of governance, no wonder reduced likelihood exists in the use of information even when acquired.

Nations are judged in our life time, not in eternity. The Bible documents the ways in which nations are judged. Natural disaster and war are to be characteristic in the world according to the Olivet Discourse. Poor judgment, the exercise of poor decision-making by leaders of nations, a problem well documented in biblical accounts: Nebuchadnezzar, Saul, David, etc. God renders futile the judgment of those that are distanced from Him. Such was the case with Nebuchadnezzar, his nephew, and pagan nations surrounding Israel. The degree to which the creature is worshipped rather than the Creator, the nation slips into paganism and abominable practices that reduce the health and well-being of the people that inhabit those nations---as witnessed in the collapse of civilization. God establishes nations in an effort to get our attention as can be seen in Acts 17; Psalms 2; and Psalms 144 to name a few. Only where God is acknowledged is there Liberty for the individual. Where the Spirit of the Lord is, there is liberty!

Festering Elements

Complicating our notions of governance exists at least two festering elements that have created mental and emotional boundaries to the public policy options, and rendered the U.S. prodigal status. These persistent sores on the soul of the nation shape how problems are perceived and what solutions are deemed appropriate. A two prong complication thwarts our progress. The difficulty comes from the erosion of biblical understanding, but with a twist. This twist instrumentally leads to futility of effort individually and collectively as a nation. The two prong difficulty of which I speak has historical roots that are felt today in the form of policy spirals, perhaps the best example were early discussions about the Iraqi conflict , an issue that will serve as prime illustration of the argument of this book. The complication is so hidden that unless you trace back the history of policy conversation domestically and internationally, it is possible to completely miss what the underlying framework of policy narrative is that shapes governance to date. The demonstrable support for entertaining the theoretical explanation offered here can be seen in past domestic debate over an international issue seeing the Iraq war un-win-able, not militarily but in the nature of thinking made evident by Congressional debate, media coverage and academic compromise. Let me explain by first taking you to seemingly completely unrelated issues out of time.

The two events are slavery and the Jewish holocaust. Each event reveals poor handling of opportunities for the church global to present a biblically sound response to issues of governance. These two historical events demonstrate the adversity of church confusion and silence which served to plant seeds sprouting government decision-making and programmatic policy response, domestically and internationally.

Let's take the first event, slavery. That is when the church was divided on opinion about the merits of owning slaves. This situation from a policy perspective is well discussed by Stephen Carter's work entitled, *God's Name in Vain*.[11] Public discourse reveals that the role God was relegated to in public decision-making and political strategizing. The second event was the Jewish holocaust. This is when the church worldwide ignored the mass extermination of Jews in Europe. Of course, each of these events is well documented. Each is a defining scar on this country and has muted collective voices that may have otherwise understood need to Acknowledge God in the Decisions of State.

What was the scar of slavery? Well, slavery left the scars of a demographically driven cycle of guilt and excuse-making within the opposing political camps, each in their own way reinforcing notions of multiculturalism and rejecting the standards of the Founders of this nation---standards that originated with their understanding of God and yielding a rather cynical kind of conversation in the public square and in intellectual circle. These are depictions of self-interest articulated by a liberal cast of scholars, the position of which is well articulated by Rogers M. Smith, author of *Civic Ideals*. In his book, the author makes the following observation in his introduction. He says,

> Today, Martin Luther King, *Jr.'s* dream of an integrated nation seems not only remote but undesirable to many black and white Americans. Proposals for immigration restriction abound, and controversies rage over the lines that should be drawn between aliens and citizens. American cities crackle with explosive tensions among Latinos, Korean-Americans, West Indians, Asian Indians, Jews, and many other groups, not just "blacks" and "whites"; and disputes over multiculturalism, hate speech, and so-called Femi-Nazis reverberate throughout the land. In these times little justification may be needed for a study of American

citizenship laws that pays special attention to issues of race, ethnicity, and gender. The relevance of the central thesis of this book now seems all too plain. In the ensuing pages, I show that through most of U.S. history, lawmakers pervasively and unapologetically structured U.S. citizenship in terms of illiberal and undemocratic racial, ethnic and gender hierarchies, for reasons rooted in basic, enduring imperatives of political life. [12]

Smith goes on to say,

> [Those] inegalitarian terms encompass some very different ideological systems to be sure; but in the U.S., beliefs in white Anglo-Saxon Protestant male superiority notoriously tend to cluster together, and I saw at least one element they had in common. Against liberal and democratic republican views describing citizenship as a human creation that ought to rest on the consent of all involved, these positions all assigned political identities—including full citizenship with eligibility for voting rights and the highest political offices-on the basis of such ascribed characteristics as race, gender, are the usually unaltered nationality and religion into which people were born. Thus I rested my book, and other early writings drawn from the research for *it*, on a framework that added what I first called ethno-cultural, and then inegalitarian ascriptive traditions of Americanism to the liberal and republican strands that other scholars featured. In place of the common portrait of America as the preeminent liberal democratic republic, with a political culture characterized by conflicts between the beneficiaries of liberal property rights and the democratic masses, I began to work out a more apparently irrational picture. In it, to be sure, political conflicts stemming from tensions inherent in capitalist market institutions and in liberal democratic values abounded. But many Americans also defined their core political identities in terms of their race, gender, religion, ethnicity, and culture. They warred passionately and often successfully against every force and faction that threatened to give the U.S. citizenry a different cast. The reasons for those passions, moreover, lay within the divided heart of American civic identity, in ways that time has altered but never destroyed. [13]

Smith's argument is that American civic life has been designed to "further, 'liberal' corporate economic interests, usually controlled by white men, rather than the interests and aspirations of all."

Stephen L. Carter's book, *God's Name in Vain*,[14] discusses the policy position on the part of politicized Christians: Abolitionists versus Providentialists. Quoting the historian Don Fehrenbacher, Carter writes:

> ...(T)he reason slavery was able to persist for so many decades was that those supporting it were moved by interest whereas those opposing it were moved by sentiment. In other words, the slaveholders would actually be affected in their daily lives by the discontinuance of the institution, whereas the abolitionists, by and large, did not suffer any personal consequences if slavery continued. It is an uneasy truth of history that materialism tends to trump idealism, even though subsequent events often prove that the idealists were right all along. Much human misery could have been avoided had enough others, at key moments in the past, spun political interest out of idealistic sentiment.[15]

According to Carter,

> One force that can weave sentiment into interest is religion, for religion, at least in its Western model, tends to point the believer away from the material and toward the transcendent. The Western religions teach their adherents to put God first, to take a moral understanding and make of it a rule by which to live; in Fehrenbacher's terms, to take that which is mere sentiment and, for God's sake, elevate it into interest.[16]

In assessing the role of the church in the public policy issue of slavery, Carter presents the historic question, *"Why was holding slaves wrong?"* In examining the sermons of Charles Finney who he describes as "considered by some as the greatest abolitionist preacher of them all," was an unapologetic Christian evangelist who mixed the passion of his antislavery convictions with the fervor of the tent meeting. In answering that question, Carter states,

> ...For Charles Finney, as for most of the abolitionists, the reason was simple: The Bible commands Christians to love their neighbors as themselves. To The antislavery preachers, the contradiction was so obvious as to need little argument. What the South was doing, the Bible forbade; and the responsibility of the Christians in the North—so the abolitionists insisted---was to end what the Reverend Theodore Parker, another prominent anti-slavery preacher, called " this plague-spot of slavery---curse to our industry, our education, our politics, and our religion."[17]

The dominant question prevailed, *"Is the only Christian responsibility to preach the gospel to slaves?"* which captured the point of focus of debate between Christians of that time.[18]

Competing Voices---*Stage Left*

Organized interests on the part of ethnicity, race and religion over time have led to a basic acceptance of multiple cultures and their trappings. As a consequence, this pattern of reasoning opened the way for justifying eclecticism---the idea that all philosophies, religions, and gods are created equal. The characteristics of which will be elaborated upon in upcoming chapters. The undermining of Christian doctrine and the rise of corporatist service provision has been the lasting reminder of ethnic and racial bouts.

But, beyond the dynamics of competing ethnic, racial, and religious groups that have taken up residence legally and illegally here, there is yet another scar on the political landscape of the United States due to the position of the Church.

The Holocaust left the scar of distrust in the institution of the church and clergy worldwide generally; and, it thoroughly disillusioned the Jewish community in America. This disillusionment was not without good reason. In the words of Sam Harris, author of a New York Times Best Seller entitled, *The End of the Faith: Religion, Terror and the Future of Reason*, makes the following statement:

> [But] the truly sinister complicity of the church came in its willingness to open its genealogical records to the Nazis and thereby enable them to trace the extent of a person's Jewishness. [19]

Harris quotes Guenther Lewy, a historian who maintains,

> The very question of whether the [Catholic] Church should lend its help to the Nazi state in sorting out people of Jewish descent was never debated. On the contrary, "We have always unselfishly worked for the people without regard to gratitude or ingratitude," a priest wrote in Klerusblatt in September 1934. "We shall all also do our best to help in this service to the people." And the cooperation of the Church in this matter continued right through the war years, when the price of being Jewish was no longer dismissal from a government job and loss of livelihood, but deportation and outright physical destruction. [20]

Harris concludes this part of his book with the following:

My purpose in this chapter has been to intimate, in as concise a manner as possible, some of the terrible consequence that have arisen, logically and inevitably, out of Christian faith. Unfortunately, this catalog of horrors could be elaborated upon indefinitely. Auschwitz, the Cathar heresy, the witch hunts---these phrases signify depths of human depravity and human suffering that would surely elude description were a writer to set himself no other task. As I have cast a very wide net in the present chapter, I can only urge Readers who may feel they have just been driven past a roadside accident at full throttle to consult the literature on these subjects.

Such extracurricular studies will reveal that the history of Christianity is principally a story of mankind's misery and ignorance rather than of its requited love of God. While Christianity has few living inquisitors today, Islam has many."[21]

The animosity expressed above is similar to that of others who see secularism as of primary import in the United States. It is only in the separation of church and state that this Jewish contingency can feel assured that the devastation that happened in Germany would not be permitted to happen in the United States. Not unlike Hamlet's mom washing compulsively, trying to get the blood off of her hands, the United States seen as a person with a guilty conscience suggests that our nation has found solace in intellectualizing its problems. The conscience center which would be the church has not maintained credibility because of its inability to come to one unified conclusion about slavery when it was underway; and, the church global did not defend the Jews during the Holocaust.

Yet, another hurdle presents itself. The very capable brain trust---the very intelligentsia of our nation is charted by secular Jewish intellectuals, who are at odds with God and that support continued secularization of our society.

The Islamic threat is not just physical attacks on our nation. It is also represents a charge against secularism, a secularism that has also dominated our approach to terrorist activity. The response of secularists is that all conversations about "god" must be squelched if there is to be any hope of peace. The politicians, however, see "god-talk" as translatable into votes. So, their political conversations are courting the church crowd. Internationally, the charge against democracy is that it is secular, and it is in an elemental form that the state department speaks of attempts to install a form of democracy in Iraq, a Muslim nation.

Not inconsequentially, characteristics of altruism, forgiveness, leisure, national character—sensitivity to others, awareness and responsibility, awareness of purpose abounds only in that which is valued. We as a nation must confront our personal and collective sins and return to the God of the Holy Bible.[22]

The most recent threat to secular notions has been the introduction of "Faith Based" Initiatives. In response to that thinking, coupled with radical fascist Islamic attacks on our nation, those who wish to divorce any conversations about religion from the market place of ideas have been able to arouse public sentiment. Religion is the problem, they say.

There are those who are too angry, disillusioned, or fearful to entertain acknowledgement of God and this situation results in bitterness. The implications are discussed in the next chapter. For now, it is important to understand that there is a point of intersection between public policy process and the concerns spawned by the Providence of God.

In essence, we are to have correct understanding and focus upon God so that we may mirror His attributes. We are to do this to His honor and glory. This is not simply a pleasantry. Right focus----Acknowledging God----is a vanishing point that puts all other aspects of our individual and collective lives into right perspective.

Since our Constitutional Republic structure of governance assumes prerequisite character traits that are to be shared by government decision-makers, one can say that **the sovereignty of the United States and the well-being of the rest of the nations of the world become jeopardized when our leaders fail to acknowledge God in the decisions of state.** This happens because the principle of self-governance rests upon the notion that a self-controlled people can make right decisions. Without the self-control, notions of right and wrong would not be enforceable. The self-control of which I speak is a gift of the Holy Spirit who is given to instruct, convict, and strengthen the believer. From the founding of our nation, the assumption prevailed that God-fearing men would operate in obedience to the law. This is important. To be unscrupulous would undermine the fabric of governance. Historically, references to character were paramount. Folks were to attest as to whether the person was "God fearing." Reinforcing that notion, the law of the land would rest upon the Ten Commandments, God's law. Further understood, the Ten Commandments would exist as the standard of governance. The positive result of this structure remained evident to all.

All nations recognize the uniqueness of those nations that operate with this biblical standard. With conscience to dictate and honorable behavior as the norm, the failure to operate conscientiously results in shunning, historically. Furthermore, moral behavior was seen a direct product of Christian upbringing.

Another historical aspect of governance in the United States was the role of the citizen. The constituency was to be literate. Literacy remained key because citizens must be able to read the word of God to discern good from evil. *de Tocqueville* spoke of this phenomenon of the role the church played in America. At the time, it was clearly understood that both prudence and diligence were directly linked to faith in God of the Holy Bible. It was (and should continue to be assumed) that individuals have the power to choose good over evil and that any evil behavior brought forth its own judgment. With the hand of Providence guiding the nation, self-interest could be seen as served best by good. Wise, prudent choices were a result of obedience to God's laws. Character shaped by the fear of God established the standard for governance.

In our current era of eclecticism where even much of the institution of the Church wavers in its allegiance to the inerrancy of Holy Scripture, it is apparent that discomfort is at its highest with exposure to the Holy Bible. The Holy Bible is the dividing line for our nation as well as the dividing line for the institutional mechanisms of the Church.

The real problem that underpins multiculturalism is a bitter futility of thought focusing upon human beings to the point of conceptual expulsion of God. The pillars of futility that result from that expulsion are identity, exclusivity, and disillusionment. I repeat. The real problem that underpins multiculturalism is a bitter futility of thought that focuses upon human beings to the point of utter irrationality, mania, accompanying all conceptual attempts to expulse *God.*

Decoding the Pattern of Futility

The original prodigals were Adam and Eve. They gave birth to a next generation prodigal, Cain. Cain is famous for committing the first murder. The following is an account of the history of Cain and Abel, from Genesis Chapter 4.

> And Adam knew Eve his wife; and she conceived and bore Cain, and said, "I have gotten a man from the LORD." And she again bore his brother Abel. And Abel was a keeper of sheep, but Cain was a tiller of the ground. And in process of time it came to pass that Cain brought of the fruit of the ground an offering unto the LORD. And Abel also brought of the firstlings of his flock and of the fat thereof. And the LORD had respect unto Abel and to his offering; but unto Cain and to his offering He had not respect. And Cain was very wroth, and his countenance fell. And the LORD said unto Cain, "Why art thou wroth? And why is thy countenance fallen? If thou doest well, shalt thou not be accepted? And if thou doest not well, sin lieth at the door. And unto thee shall be his desire, and thou shalt rule over him." And Cain talked with Abel his brother; and it came to pass, when they were in the field, that Cain rose up against Abel his brother and slew him. And the LORD said unto Cain, "Where is Abel thy brother?" And he said, "I know not. Am I my brother's keeper?" And He said, "What hast thou done? The voice of thy brother's blood crieth unto Me from the ground. And now art thou cursed from the earth, which hath opened her mouth to receive thy brother's blood from thy hand. When thou tillest the ground, it shall not henceforth yield unto thee her strength. A fugitive and a vagabond shalt thou be on the earth." And Cain said unto the LORD, "My punishment is greater than I can bear. Behold, Thou hast driven me out this day from the face of the earth, and from Thy face shall I be hid; and I shall be a fugitive and a vagabond on the earth. And it shall come to pass that everyone who findeth me shall slay me." And the LORD said unto him, "Therefore whosoever slayeth Cain, vengeance shall be taken on him sevenfold." And, the LORD set a mark upon Cain, lest any finding him should kill him. And Cain went out from the presence of the LORD, and dwelt in the land of Nod to the east of Eden. And Cain knew his wife, and she conceived and bore Enoch. And he built a city, and called the name of the city after the name of his son, Enoch.[23]

Many interesting commentaries exist on Chapter Four of Genesis, but for purposes of this discussion I wish to point out a few major elements to this history that have bearings on the issue individual judgment and societal decision-making, the first being that forgiveness comes from right reconciliation with God. That is the point of this passage.

Prodigal Behavior Fueled by Disillusionment and Bitterness

The importance of forgiveness is expressed by Dallas Willard, who says, "...when we are personally injured our world does not suddenly become our injury. We have a larger view of our life and our place in God's world. We see God; we see ourselves in his hands. We see our injurer as more than that one who has imposed on us or hurt us. We recognize his humanity, his pitiful limitations (shared with us), and we also see him under God. This vision, and the grace that comes with it, enables the prayer: "Father forgive them, for they do not really understand what they are doing." And in fact they don't, as Jesus well knew when he prayed this prayer over his murderers."[24]

In Genesis 4, we see that Cain was not to treat Abel right because Cain was not in right relation with God. Instead of correcting his relation with God, Cain committed murder. In the above situation, the impact was murder, evidence of breakdown directly attributable to distance from God.

Prodigal Behavior Rooted in Resentment toward Groups, Good, and God

Cain resented God because God would not accept what Cain was willing to offer Him. Cain knew that the nature of the offering God sought was not just arbitrary but was to be a constant reminder of the promise of the redemptive work of Christ. Blood was required to cover sin and its consequences requiring animal sacrifice-- not plant life, fig leaves or vegetable matter. Recognizing that God was willing to accept Abel's offering because it met what was required by God, an angered Cain decided to destroy the Good to hurt God. The grievance was not resolved but festered up to the point of murder.

The critical element is the moral erosion of our nation that is a consequence of our distance from God. Morality is not simply a human contrivance essential to right judgment. C. S. Lewis once observed,

> ...When a man is getting better he understands more and more clearly the evil that is still left in him. When a man is getting worse, he understands his own badness less and less. A moderately bad man knows he is not very good: a thoroughly bad man thinks he is all right. This is common sense, really. You

understand sleep when you are awake, not while you are sleeping. You can see
mistakes in arithmetic when your mind is working properly: while you are making
them you cannot see them. You can understand the nature of drunkenness when
you are sober, not when you are drunk. Good people know about both good and
evil: bad people know about neither.[25]

Admittedly, the link between right relations with God to something like the public debate
is easily overlooked because our political debate is not geared toward considering God's
point of view. Failing to take captive our ideas by seeing them through a biblical lens is
what makes us more susceptible individually and as a nation to a myriad of difficulties---
including international blackmail.

      Worldwide, there is a diabolical progression afoot seen most clearly in Europe,
the cycle is one of secularized tolerance, followed by increased societal decadence
[including abortion, homosexuality, child molestation, and worse], all of which is then
followed by purported Islamic piety, and finally, population growth among Islamists with
the goal of demographic dominance

      What Cain needed was deliverance. This is what modern-day Cain needs also.
That is what nations of the world need that carry the same traits as Cain possessed, that of
harboring malice and envy. The deliverance cycle follows:

Deliverance Cycle for the Prodigal

      There is a natural progression from adherence to Biblical principles to that of
moral clarity in decisions made by individuals. With discernment—a spiritual gift from
God—new ideas emerge, inventions. Those inventions afford prosperity, both
intellectual and financial in the sense that one acquires the ability from God to know how
to maximize the use of the skills and resources God has provided. Problems tend to
emerge for the individual when they become so engaged with the gifts of prosperity that
they distance themselves from the gift Giver who is God. At this point idolatry becomes
evident as more and more time, devotion, and resources become redirected toward the
maintenance of those gifts. As Forgetfulness of God becomes more and more frequent,
there is a decline in the life of the individual—not necessarily immediately noticeable,
but a decline nonetheless. Faithlessness sets in made most evident by the level of fear
the individual has about day-to-day occurrences. God in His mercy may allow the
individual to gradually decline or He may most mercifully allow the individual to "hit the

wall" sort of speak so that the person may turn back to God. Turning back to God is what repentance means. Repentance means returning to one's right place in relationship with God and it also means a restoration to one's right mind. The deliverance is from idolatry. Idolatry defined is anything that becomes more important in one's life than reverence for God. Once deliverance occurs, sanity returns. With sanity comes moral clarity. The Personal Deliverance Cycle follows:

For the Individual

Following Christ/Adherence to Biblical Principles → Moral Clarity→ Invention→ Prosperity→Forgetfulness of God→Decline→Cry Out to God in Repentance→Deliverance→Moral Clarity, Etc.--The cycle goes on.

A similar process deliverance cycle occurs with nations. Nations that have cultures influenced by biblical principles bring forth institutions and persons of authority that have a higher incidence of moral clarity made evident by the degree of adherence to the law. It is in those societies that invention occurs to preserve life. Preservation of human life becomes priority because it is understood that human beings are made in the image of God. Diligent search for means to honor God and support that which the population understands to be desired of God yields prosperity. In modern times, we have seen what happens when prosperous pursuits displace acknowledgment of God. There are a number of adverse conditions that are not responded to with the moral clarity required to preserve quality of life for the population. If the difficulties confronting the nation become severe enough, some may cry out to God in repentance and then intercede in behalf of the nation. Restoration of the believers in Christ to their "First Love" brings restoration to the church. The church restored can welcome the move of God for Revival in the entire land. This National Deliverance Cycle is as follows:

For the Nation

Aggregates of Individuals Following Christ/Adherence to Biblical Principles → Moral Clarity→ Invention→ Prosperity→Forgetfulness of God→Decline→Cry Out to God in Repentance→REVIVAL→Deliverance→Moral Clarity, Etc.--The cycle goes on.

What is really going on in our world that makes deliverance a necessity?

Well, God says,

> The wrath of God is being revealed from heaven against all godlessness and wickedness of men who suppress the truth by their wickedness, since what may be known about God is plain to them, because God has made it plain to them. for since the creation of the world God's invisible qualities—His eternal power and divine nature---have been clearly seen, being understood from what has been made so that men are without excuse. For although they knew God, they neither glorified Him as God nor gave thanks to Him, *but their thinking became futile* and their foolish hearts were darkened. Although they claimed to be wise, they became fools and exchanged the glory of the immortal God for images made to look like mortal man and birds and animals and reptiles. Therefore God gave them over in the sinful desires of their hearts to sexual impurity for the degrading of their bodies with one another. They exchanged the truth of God for a lie, and worshiped and served created things rather than the Creator---who is forever praised. Amen. [26]

God's View Versus Man's View

The willingness of professing believers to operate as if all religions, philosophies, and gods are created equal has further exposed our nation to vulnerability. With right standing in God, we can withstand all of our enemies. Indeed, it is only because of God's grace to us that we have not been utterly consumed. God has blessed and continues to bless our nation.

Climatic warning shots, however, continue. God does have something to say to us. What follows is an account from Leviticus 26:14-18, taken from the Amplified Bible. God says,

> *"But if you will not hearken to Me and will not do all these commandments, and if you spurn and despise My statutes, and if your soul despises and rejects My ordinances, so that you will not do all My commandments, but break My covenant, I will do this: I will appoint over you [sudden] terror (trembling, trouble), even consumption and fever that consume and waste the eyes and make the [physical] life pine away. You shall sow your seed in vain, for your enemies shall eat it."*
>
> *" I [the Lord] will set My face against you and you shall be defeated and slain before your enemies; they who hate you shall rule over you; you shall flee when no one pursues you. And if in spite of all this you still will not listen and be obedient to Me, then I will chastise and discipline you seven times more for your sins."[27]*

Prolonged Prodigal Status Yields Rebellion that Can Resist Repentance

Grief often expresses itself in retaliation rather than conscious soul-searching and repentance that can heal the pain. Cain could have chosen repentance but he chose not to.

Prolonged Prodigal Status Yields Rebellion that Rejects Communion

Because Cain was unrepentant, he remained distanced from God. That distance became reinforced by displacement geographically. Commentators point to his eviction to East of Eden as the beginning of the building of "a *City.*" Cain and his family busied themselves making "civilization." Enoch, the name of this city, means "initiation," and was "symbolic of the new city where Cain would try to mitigate his curse." It is noteworthy that mitigation was pursued via civility and not through reconciliation with God.

Yet another negative outworking of the Cain and Abel history is the erroneous view of God as existing primarily to help people get what they desire to have either emotionally or materially. In our age, according to one author, "the object of religion sounds like capitalist consumerism – acquiring the goods of this life,"[28] I would further add that at the very core of error, the problem is anger.

As far as the initial disillusionment is concerned, Chambers maintains:

> Disillusionment means that there are no more false judgments in life. To be undeceived by of much suffering in human life. It works in this way – if we love a human being and do not love God, we demand of him every perfection and every rectitude, and when we do not get it we become cruel and vindictive; we are demanding of a human being that which he or she cannot give. There is only one being who can satisfy the last aching abyss of the human heart, and that is the Lord Jesus Christ. That is why our Lord is apparently so severe regarding every human relationship.[29]

Thought constraint exists because at the root of secular scholarship there is a preoccupation with limiting conversation to the ideas of men as mentioned earlier. This *equi-finality, constant action with little to no significant improvement of result,* is fostered by hampered vision, delusion, and guilt. Lack of repentance reinforces error in the form of misspecification of problem, politically convenient definition of circumstances that range from completely intolerable for some to mere nuisance for others. Resentment and disillusionment fosters derivative thought. Thought derived from some point that misses the mark of truthfulness about a situation. It is my contention that missing the mark is missing God and that means missing Truth.

"The concept of idolatry is not that simple. What happened was that people realized that humans needed to be guided and governed by some code of conduct, but they were insistent that whatever authority they accept upon themselves should not encroach upon their personal desires. They therefore developed a system of religion which they could manipulate to accommodate their needs. A man-made god served this purpose very well, because if conditions were such that the prevailing religion interfered too much with their lives, it was a minor task to fashion a new idol through which they could establish more accommodating rules. They were indeed capable of reasoning to the truth just as Abraham did, but realization of the truth would have made them subject to the sovereignty of the true God, and this would have impinged on their comfort. Their self-centeredness and self-indulgence thus blinded them to the truth, much as anyone's judgment is distorted by personal interests. People believed in idols because this is what they wanted to believe and, as so often happens, emotion overruled intellect.....To the degree that one possesses *chesed* (kindness), to that degree he can accept God as his sovereign, and subject himself to the will of God. Abraham's selflessness was so absolute that he became a "bearer" of the Divine presence. ....If a person is motivated primarily by what will satisfy his personal desires, he is practicing the essence of idolatry. One can even be technically observant of many *mitzvos*, but to the degree that self-indulgence is one's goal in life, to that degree one is guilty of idolatry."[30]

THERE IS A PATTERN OF IRRATIONALITY (FUTILITY) ASSOCIATED WITH DISTANCING OURSELVES FROM GOD. ONCE THAT PATTERN OF DEPRAVED IRRATIONALITY IS INITIATED, GOD SAYS THAT THE INDIVIDUAL THAT SUCCUMBS WILL NOT EVEN RECOGNIZE IT.

Francis Bacon, the scientist that gave us the scientific method, was a Christian. The beauty of the scientific method was the ability to determine the Truthfulness of conclusion, the process of pursuing truth allowed for discovery---macro explanations of reality that we call theories while being tested for truthfulness, and laws once we recognize that what we discovered is "*True.*" It is no mistake to find in this age of resistance to the "idea" of absolute truth, an accompanying disdain for the tools used to assess/test the truthfulness of claims. An era where the starting point, the point of departure of argument can be anywhere including on occasion at the point of truth, but only haphazardly and with greater infrequency as we become further removed from the God of the Bible, and are left to the futility of our thinking and the degeneracy of each subsequent act.

The Problem of Derivative Thought

Derivative thought is thinking that begins with a fragmented element of the Truth as if it were the whole truth. Derivative thought is what results in government policy spirals described in this text as the building of large bureaucratic activity---public, private, nonprofit, nongovernmental or mixed---designed to address the mere symptoms of much more fundamental problems. Because the solutions strategies miss the mark in the first place, the results at best are temporarily beneficial, contradictory, and unstable for the society to move forward. This problem is keen in the developed world and is the primary obstacle to nation building in the less developed world.

The consequence of being off center is empirically discernible. The *Holy Bible* offers the plumb line for assessing deficiency in understanding. Fundamentally, those who do not share a biblical mindset can nonetheless recognize Truth; it is knowable, just not routinely or consciously exercisable in the absence of one's acknowledgment of God. A biblical understanding of humanity suggests that man is not evolving but rather devolving in his capacity to think as he denies God. One biblical scholar has even suggested that given the explained and otherwise misplaced artifacts of the past such as the pyramids, we can see that since the great cataclysmic event of the Flood, man has lost much ground and indeed has failed to recover intellectually. Humanity is still staggering from that cataclysmic exhibition of God's wrath.

More recently, we have seen evidence of God's wrath. Natural disasters are increasing in both frequency and severity throughout the world. They are worsening the conditions of underdeveloped regions where social plight abounds. The aftermath of natural disasters bears both external political and national security implications. Such devastated places become the breeding ground for transnational criminal activity and provide safe harbor for enemies of the United States. Meanwhile, here in the United

States, we forget that we too are susceptible to such forms of natural calamity including the dreaded tsunami. Indeed, researchers have found that the combination of population density, natural wealth density, and aging infrastructure coupled with natural calamity yield much greater loss.

Failed reasoning at multiple levels was evident in the response to New Orleans, Louisiana in 2005. From a purely public management standpoint, the contamination of dependency upon modern conveniences and the interruption of such conveniences when natural disaster hits has rendered the public ill prepared. Municipal and state governments have an added burden of already over-stretched budgets, untrained volunteer base, nonprofit fiefdoms, and federal bureaucratic red tape. If one were to examine societal indicators from a biblically informed perspective, it would be evident that social dissipation costs. It costs in reduced quality of life. It costs in greater exposure to internal and external risks. It costs in terms of clarity of judgment about response. There are only two postures available:

"If God be God, serve God. If Baal be god, serve Baal" [31]

Figure 1.1 presents the cycle of deliverance for the individual.

Figure 1.1

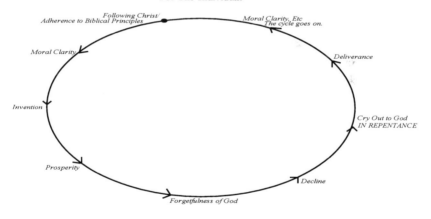

The Deliverance Cycle
For The Individual

A similar cycle exists as shown in Figure 1.2 for nations, individuals in aggregate constituting the "body politic". The difference is that "truly delivered" individuals gain freedom from repeated moral failure, and are able gain ever-increasing spiritual ground for whole, wholesome, i.e. "holy", living. Collective incidence of such repentance spells national revival. [32]

Figure 1.2

The Deliverance Cycle
For The Nation

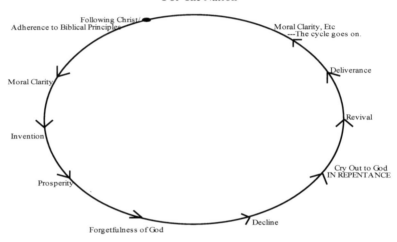

What Moral Clarity Yields: A Bit of History

The first attempt at the experiment of loose governance failed. It was under the Articles of Confederation that the potential threat of regional interests surfaced. To have colonies devise their economic policies independent of each other meant that the colonies could become and did indeed become susceptible to competition between each other, establishing trade relations to the detriment of the economic well-being of the colonies. The founders saw the need to have both the executive and legislative branches involved in foreign policy for federative concerns more so than any issues of one branch of federal government dominating another. The thinking influenced by their understanding of human nature as revealed in the Holy Bible translated into principled action. As a consequence of recognizing the natural fallen status of humanity, "checks and balances" were introduced into the system of governance. The founders wanted to avoid the monarchial analogy of "King" for the leadership of this new country. Hence the term presidency was settled upon so that there would be a since of shared representative responsibility over the decisions of state. The president was elected to preside over the affairs of state as a manger/executor of the will of the people rather than as a ruler. It was the federative threat, that loose and internally inconsistent network of competing colonies that led to the ultimate signing of the United States Constitution.

FIGHTS ORCHESTRATED AGAINST THE CONSTITUTION OF THE UNITED STATES REPRESENT REJECTION OF THE BIBLICAL UNDERSTANDING OF THE NATURE OF FALLEN MANKIND AND THE NEED FOR LAW AS ASCRIBED BY THE TEN COMMANDMENTS.

The biblically principled document, what we call the United States Constitution, foundationally formulated by those who acknowledged God-ordained justice as articulated in the Declaration of Independence, was written to assure order where it had been absent under the confederative system; and, moved beyond simplistic notions to biblically sound understanding of the nature of humanity. In response to that understanding, "checks and balances" were established as a direct response to concerns about the corruptibility of power, a characteristic associated with our fallen nature. In addition, the founders wanted to avoid the making of a new aristocracy, skillfully attempting to divest the nation of this potential problem by delimiting the rights and responsibilities of the presidency and Congress.

What about the quality of decision making during times of crisis?

Well, from time to time, there has been political debate about what truly constitutes a national threat and "national interest." The founders had sharp views concerning these issues. Indeed, foreign policy from the perspective of the Founders appears reflected in the constitutional provisions for both the executive and legislative branches of government. The basis for constitutional provisions described in detail in the

Federalist Papers provides written documentation of the thought process by the architects of the country's system of governance. A very brief summary of contents follows. Consider the thought processes at work with these underpinnings of our constitutional structure.

Federalist Papers No. 3 and 4 focused on response to international hostilities confronting the country. Federalist Paper No. 7 speaks of wars in response to atrocities breaching "moral obligations and justice." Federalist Paper No. 23 and 46 argue for unlimited defense and fiscal powers; while, No. 75 explores the ability to make treaties. Those Papers reflect the early need for the new country to establish itself as a political entity in the aftermath of the War of Independence. The colonies were attempting to establish collective identity while simultaneously attempting to establish sovereign authority in the international arena. What sovereign authority implies is prerogative in terms of action and response internationally. Juggling notions of freedom and limitations are required to hold the country together even though they have contradictory tendencies. Order was difficult with rebellion as the cornerstone foundation for stability.

Ultimately, at the heart of foreign policy is the concern for declaration of war and peace. Having recognized the capriciousness with which the monarchs of the past had operated in Europe, much attention focused on the establishment of war powers and the accompanying system of checks and balances. As such, the President and Congress have specific roles and responsibilities in the foreign policy making process. Foreign policy is defined here as those strategic mechanisms that are employed to protect U.S. national interest in the international arena, primarily by means of diplomacy but also with the use of military intervention. The foreign policy tools include the use of treaties, the appointment and receipt of ambassadors to and from foreign countries for purposes of diplomacy, powers granted to the President of the United States by virtue of Article II of the Constitution of the United States. Congress has the power to approve treaties, to declare war, to create, maintain, and regulate the armed forces, and to regulate international trade. Both the President and Congress share responsibilities in foreign policy and national defense. The pattern has been for Congress to submit to the leadership of the president in issues of national defense. As Commander and Chief, the

Presidents of the United States collectively have initiated military force around the world on over 160 occasions compared to Congress' official declaration of war 5 times. The relationship between the President and Congress has been best described as a "system of overlapping competing powers" where the executive and legislative branches of government are constitutionally required to cooperate in the protection of the national interest from *any* and *all* international threat.

Examining Secularized Responses

Fast forwarding from the past, we see that foreign and domestic policy becomes philosophically and politically intertwined. The change, built on the operative belief that all religions, philosophies, and gods are created equal, is called "eclecticism."

Displacement of Biblical Understanding by Eclecticism Reinforces Prodigal Status

Eclecticism is the product of horizontal thinking. It focuses on social manipulation of many rather than the vertical depth required to answer any of the profound questions of life--questions emanating from our separation from God, and hence the separation of our humanity from its true self. The challenge to the domestic concerns stem frequently from the move to compartmentalize faith, to separate it from basic functions of governance. Individual decisions determine the day regarding how one wishes to place oneself in the context of controversy over the inerrancy of scripture. Decision is required because the God of the Bible through the convicting presence of His Holy Spirit will not allow us to remain neutral.

Eclecticism is a kind of religious multiculturalism. Make no mistake about it, the Holy Bible is the dividing line for our nation. The division within the nation has implications for how the United States will fair in the international arena. We will return to this issue in a later chapter. For now let it suffice it to say that decisions rooted in biblical principles require divergence from secular frames of reference that will have internal and international implications. Scrutiny suggests that eclecticism violates the boundaries that distinguish true Christianity from other religions and cults. Bloesch in his book, Faith and Its Counterfeits reminds us,

"If we examine the Bible carefully, we see that no where are the people of God urged to accommodate or adjust their beliefs to those of surrounding culture, the Old Testament prophets were especially adamant that the religion of Israel be kept free from the taint of the idolatrous religions of the Canaanites and other tribes. Elijah, in opposing the attempts of Ahab and Jezebel to come to terms with Baal worship, spoke for all the prophets: "How long will you waver between two opinions? If the LORD is God, follow Him; but if Baal is God, follow him." [33]

ACTION POINT

What does this mean for the exercise of biblically-informed statesmanship in prodigal societies?

Obviously, not everyone agrees with our biblical view of the world. To be "Salt" and "Light" in this world, suggests that it is not sufficient for those who share a biblical worldview to limit conversation to ourselves. Providentially, the role of research is to uncover Truth. This is good! But, "bad news" also exists. *Fact is*: Finding out what is true these days can be rather elusive. At the core of the problem lies with the lack of appreciation for the whole idea of "Absolute Truth," a concept that can only be garnered from right understanding and application of the Holy Bible. Obviously, one can only establish certainty where there exists a solid understanding of what constitutes the "Plumb Line."

The clash between patterns of thought, the assumptions underlying conventional "research" versus Bible-Based --- Truth-Driven Inquiry---may appear in a number of forms.

1. The contradictions may be definitional--- conceptually, operationally, or both

2. The contradictions may be philosophical, in the sense of expressing normative ("what should be") statements

3. The contradictions may be in matter of substance, evidence of the presence or absence of what is being discussed

4. The contradictions may be in terms of severity of import of aspects of the topic and/or the repercussions associated with the presence of the key aspect being investigated

5. The contradiction may be associated with approach to investigation

6. The contradiction may suggest a notion of progress that hampers or otherwise attempts to undermine what God states as valuable

7. The contradiction may be degree of toleration entertained for the presence of the phenomenon that is under investigation

Such are just a few situations where that which constitutes previously published information from "reputable" sources renders verdicts, implied if not articulated, serving to diminish what God sanctifies, and celebrate that which God hates.

What is required in such circumstances is a "well-reasoned" response that points to the implications of the path or reasoning upon which researchers are moving. It requires the development of a word picture substantiated by reason, inductively, deductively, or both, to recast the question so that others will find no fault in the description. Such was the strategy Christ Jesus used with the lawyer who inquired, "Who is my neighbor?"

In research the word picture would be substantiated by numbers or other concrete evidence. The framework that I have most appreciated is this:

1. Statement of what has come before.

2. Schools of thought or points of agreement and disagreement between researchers most cited in the field with regard to the question you are investigating - [Make sure you can recite the genealogy of thought, the progression of key concepts to date and then list the derivatives that have emerged as a consequence of those patterns of thought.]

3. Specific pillars of the arguments associated with those dominant perspectives

4. Then, find one case* per school of thought (the assumption here being that there may be competing schools of thought each of which resting on premises that are antithetical to biblical understanding. Choose – just one case that reflects common place occurrence so that critics will not be able to dismiss your case as an aberration. Make sure the case you explore meets the definitional context(s) requirements of the researchers that have gone before, and proceed to describe in great detail all of the salient attributes that should be a natural outgrowth of the case if indeed the underlying assumptions being made by the prominent researchers is true. I suggest that you tackle no more than three schools of thought at a time. If there are more, make sure you address the two most prominent, ones that represent collectively approximately 90 percent of the publications as the foundational orientation of the published studies. [*By case, I am referring to a context, location, or situation that meets the terms associated with the competing school of thought in your research area. The logic is this. The credibility of an explanation rests on whether or not evidence exists pointing to an outcome that differs from what would be expected if the prevailing theory (explanation) were true.]

5. Prayerfully, identify the scriptural address of the topic you are investigating and then proceed to assess each case on the basis of the biblical principles being overlooked in the

case that would otherwise have been handled differently if conventional "wisdom" were applied: starting with how the problem is defined and then progressing to the point at which terms would be defined and measured.

Because you will have outlined the themes and propositions that are commonly understood by prominent researchers, you should go to your case and start your checklist with seeing if those things be present or absent. Then, proceed to delineate those attributes that exist but fail to be accounted for by current researchers. Once you have completed this exercise, write a summation. And, then write a paragraph of conclusions, closing with the implications and what that should mean for the direction of future research.

Biblically-informed statesmen should uncover that which is important first to God and then the consequences for humanity, challenges currently overlooked or otherwise unaddressed. This will open up the research conversation to entertain an alternative approach to viewing existing problems.

CHAPTER TWO

Acknowledging God in Public Policy Dynamics

"For although they knew God, they neither glorified him as God nor gave thanks to him, but their thinking became futile and their foolish hearts were darkened. Although they claimed to be wise, they became fools and exchanged the glory of the immortal God for images made to look like mortal man and birds and animals and reptiles.[34]*Romans 1: 21-23, Holy Bible.*

Secularized Reinforcement of Social Scars

It is important for us to examine ourselves and examine the teachers we have had in life. According to Dallas Willard, author of *The Divine Conspiracy,* the teachers we have had along the way communicated much to us substantively. We should examine what we have learned and do so in light of the Gospel of Jesus Christ to determine if there exists any error influencing us. This is one of the stages to strengthening our discipleship. In examining the influences our training has had on are ability see scholarship from God's perspective that is ability to put on the Mind of Christ, Willard would urge that we need to examine our lives to determine the teachers and teaching we have received, the ideas that were conveyed, and the impact that have potentially served as obstacles to our discipleship. By discipleship, we are referring to our student status as students of Our Lord and Savior Jesus Christ. The implications of teaching conveyed substantively, in particular, the problem of slavery, may be examined first from a secular and then from a biblical perspective.

Understanding the Trap of Secularized[35] Reinforcement of Social Scars Yielding Justification for Prodigal Status

Identity from a secular perspective yields:

- --- Identity as personal definition of oneself; as a place in this world; amongst others of like kind; value; community; or relevance given one's worldview
- ---Identity as a source of meaning; value, essence, worth
- --- Identity as who we are in relation to others
- --- Identity as the degree of shared identity with the collective aggregate
- --- Identity as empathy, as a characteristic of the progressive mindset
- --- Identity important in relation to behavior
- ----Identity that leads to prodigal behavior
- ----Identity in the example of the demoniac – analogous situation of competing voices that may ultimately result in hurt to oneself
- ---- Identity as image of who we are; as a function of whomever we wish to emulate

What would the biblical view of slavery be?

Perhaps Psalm 37 is an expression of response to the world when one is a slave. Psalm 37 says, *"Our captors asked us to sing songs."* In other words, there was outward oppression. An example of slavery associated with inward oppression is present in Psalm 107. Expressed in Psalm 107 are a number of attributes of slavery:

---the aimless wander that is never satisfied

---the prisoner that is in prison because of his rebelliousness toward God

---the fool that is trapped by his iniquities

---those caught in the travails of life, trying to earn a living

---the wicked

---the humbled

The response that works according to the Word of God is the same for each of the above scenarios.

"Then they cried out to the Lord in their trouble and He delivered them from their distress."[36]

In response to the questions of oppression, one need only read Psalm 137 to see God's answer.

God also has something to say about Justice. Isaiah 56 gives a clear description of what to expect of those that see oppression. Commonly the presence of both inward and outward oppression simultaneously feeds as a self-replicating loop. Such injustice germinates layers of complexity undermining the ability to hear gospel Truth, especially because of the role of those who professed Christ yet found slavery justifiable.

As mentioned earlier, the second point of obstruction posing a problematic element to receptivity to the Gospel is the Jewish holocaust. The Jewish Holocaust is well documented. The survivors and their families were ravaged. Disillusioned, many survivors they arrived in New York. The tragedy they lived through is not presented here by the voice of a survivor. Rather, I have chosen to call your attention to a brief account from someone who did not survive. What follows here is not an account of an adult, but rather that of a child who was murdered with countless others. We all have heard of her. Here is an observation from *The Diary of Anne Frank*, an observation made by one person who did not survive. Hear her voice.

> Have you ever heard the term 'hostages'? That's the latest punishment for saboteurs. It's the most horrible thing you can imagine. Leading citizens-- innocent people --are taken prisoner to await their execution. If the Gestapo can't find the saboteur, they simply grab five hostages and line them up against the wall. You read the announcements of their death in the paper, where they're referred to as 'fatal accidents." - October 9, 1942.[37]

Sobering, isn't it?

No wonder there are those who would prefer to seek refuge in that which remains far removed from any religious tradition in an effort to avoid vulnerability to the above. The case that can be made that part of the explanation for displacement of biblical understanding with eclecticism rests upon disillusionment in the United States. With slavery, the consequences yields a notion of "Race" as "Religion." With the Holocaust, the consequence yields secular reasoning as religion.

Challenges in Decision-Making

Identity in family, tribe, nation, territory, and way of life, as a community can be elevated from the tangible to the intangible in terms of shared faith and belief systems. These systems can reflect supra structure of worldview, expectations, aspirations, and possibilities as well as limits.

Within this notion of identity as linked to worldview, there are competing influences with the goal of posturing oneself to live. Such attachments have functional consequences. Biblically speaking, *"How can two walk together less they are agreed?"*

Identity may be based upon isolation; as dependency as child to parent or guardian; as being excluded from all other possible affiliations either as a consequence of personal choice, choices made by others within or beyond your control; or as consequence of real or imagined boundaries beyond which one does not (nor attempts to) cross.

Psychological affiliation can be viewed as a consequence of social exclusion by some and inclusion by others. Exclusion driven affiliation tends to dominate the Black experience. Socio-political hierarchy has historically established itself within the context of the relatively isolated group with limited numbers interacting with others outside the group. Then, there was a gradual opening of the group.

Group opening potentially jeopardized the power base that was once secure within the context of isolation. As a consequence, attempts were made to maintain power by projecting the continual threat of rejection by the outside so that there would be the perceived need for the original hierarchy to retain relevance/legitimacy as a protective necessity.

Then as the opening became larger, those who were located in areas that were physically isolated as well as economically had a higher likelihood of maintaining traditional hierarchical arrangements within the church – the only institution that was allowed to exist intact even through the period of slavery. Sunday was the day that one could assume the posture of a human being, created by God, who is just.

Those who could rise to position of minister had positions of influence, authority, and legitimacy. They were the most articulate and could communicate position, argument, as well as rhetorically profess the wisdom of God so much so that the slave community itself saw itself as possessing many parallels with the Israelites of the Holy Bible, a "theocracy" in search of the Promised Land.

Those who grew out of this tradition of preaching maintained a "prophetic" posture that became most prominent in the personage of Dr. Martin Luther King. The preachment of social justice and the declaration of the apparent injustices prescribed the context for public debate. The preachment of human requisites even from Malcolm X whose rhetorical approach of presumed logical conversation rather than prophetic oratory also contributed to the merging of political stance with the notion of transcendent justice.

Racial Mobilization and Estrangement

Appeasement was rendered to the Black community via the church in opposition to the alternative that was offered by the militant and attached religious element, a hybrid version of Islam for the states.

The political benefits gleaned by race had to be distributed via the church because again is was the only established entity that could maximize political benefit for the decision makers who wanted to maintain stability; and, for the hierarchy of the isolated communities, it represent those wanting to share in the benefit and politically solidify themselves on the basis of the rewards that were to be gained for the community.

As the degree of structural separation began to diminish, the psychological demarcation reinforced the rhetoric of the leadership to hold together the power base. Race, when physical barriers are eliminated, requires the establishment of psychological barriers if those who lead have had their reason for leadership authority and legitimacy has been established on the basis of rejection by the other group.

Race in the psychological realm leads to an ethnocentrism as religious fervor in the same manner as citizenship in the psychological realm leads to patriotism--- another form of allegiance that approximates religion. Ethnocentrism that exudes religious fervor is associated with charismatic leadership because there is a need for the elevation of someone to the level that approximates deification so that when seen as affiliated with the group, the individual perceives association with power. This is especially desirous among those who have perceived themselves as "down trodden." Such was the case of Germany prior to the war. Hitler charismatically established himself by rhetorically speaking to the transcendence of race to those who had perceived themselves as having nothing.

This also renders a feeling of superiority to have the "other" group believed to be inferior. Actions follow the accepted definition of reality. Actions that go unchallenged have legitimacy. Actions that become routine have attached to themselves authority. Routine actions that initially were in reaction to something deemed negative continue to persist beyond need if there are sunken costs associated with the institutions built upon the foundation of the lasting presence of the "problem."

If the problem is solved or near solved, these institutions continue because they have a means of reminding their constituency that there is a threat of reversion. Such is the case of the Black Liberation church that has become a political entity. I must state here that not all churches that are predominately Black are "Black churches," meaning Black first, and then church. Only those that are Black first and then church have made race a religion.

Those that are church, meaning body of Christ first, and then secondarily Black are real churches rather than simply religiously mobilized units. I contend that the degree to which a race is a religion is directly associated with the degree of absence of sound doctrine. The biblical reason for my position is the conversation of Jesus with the Samaritan Woman at the well. She spoke politics associated with religious affiliation. She began this conversation race question – why is it that Jesus, a member of another race, should be talking to her. I believe that Jesus was communicating something when he failed to respond to her question concerning race. We pointed to the "living water" which by the way is the reason for the church and questioned her focus of conversation. He challenged her by asking and the describing her relationships (gender) as a byproduct of not being rightly reconciled with God.

Surprise! How the problems of demographic imagery are handled within the domestic arena of the United States do have international implications. It is interesting to note that the Church has progressively lost traction of preparing the citizenry with Biblical knowledge. As a consequence, moral clarity has diminishes at an exponential rate. The impotence of the Church institutional has had enormous adverse consequence in that it represented the removal of God from the public square. As mentioned before, the first historical source of public muffling about the Divine at the national level came about during the public debate over the merits and demerits of slavery in the United States. The second historical source of muffling squelch came with the worldwide silence of the Church during the Holocaust. The two events, African slavery and the Jewish holocaust, each revealed the onerous handling of opportunities for the church global to present a biblically sound response to issues of governance. These two historical events showcasing church confusion and silence served to fertilize the nation for sprouting our current multi-culturally sensitive environment. As a consequence, government decision-making fails to produce logical programmatic policy response domestically and internationally

Again, the Islamic threat is not just physical attacks on our nation. The response of secularists is that all conversations about "god" must be squelched if there is to be any hope of peace. Political conversations are courting the church crowd. Internationally, the charge against democracy is that it is secular, and it is in an elementary form of that articulated position that the Department of State during the Bush Jr. administration speaks of installing a form of democracy in Iraq, a Muslim nation.

We as a nation must confront our personal and collective sins and return to the God of the Holy Bible. God-honoring traits are not that of "milk toast." C.S. Lewis points to the dynamic of love prescribed by God for ones enemies. He explains forgiveness and love for others as oneself.

> Now that I come to think of it, I have not exactly got a feeling of or find him [my enemy] attractive. I ought to have seen that before, because, of course, you cannot feel fond of a person by trying. Do I think well of myself, think myself a nice chap? Well, I am afraid I sometimes do … but that is not why I love myself. So loving my enemies does not apparently mean thinking them nice either. That is an enormous relief. For a good many people imagine that forgiving your enemies means making out that they are really not such bad fellows after all, when it is quite plain that they are. Go a step further. In my most clear-sighted moments not only do I not think myself a nice man, but I know that I am a very nasty one. I can look at some of the things I have done with horror and loathing. So apparently I am allowed to loathe and hat some of the things my enemies do. Now that I come to think of it, I remember Christian teachers telling me long ago that I must hate a bad man's actions, but not hate the bad man: or, as they would say, hate the sin but not the sinner.

For a long time I used to think this a silly, straw-splitting distinction: how could you hate what a man did and not hate the man? But years later it occurred to me that there was one man to whom I had being this all my life—namely myself. However much I might dislike my own cowardice or conceit or greed. I went on loving myself. There had never been the slightest difficulty about it. In fact the very reason why I hated the things was that I loved the man. Just because I loved myself, I was sorry to find that I was the sort of man who did those things. Consequently, Christianity does not want us to reduce by one atom the hatred we fee for cruelty and treachery. We ought to hate them. Not one word of what we have said about them needs to be unsaid. But it does want us to hate them in the same way in which we hate things in ourselves: being sorry that the man should have done such things, and hoping, if it is any way possible, that somehow, sometime, somewhere, he can be cured and made human again.[38]

And, what does God of the Holy Bible say,

With God as Ruler over Israel, He makes the following statements in Leviticus 26:

"Do not make idols or set up an image or a sacred stone for yourselves, and do not place a carved stone in your land to bow down before it. I am the LORD your God. (v. 1) "Observe my Sabbaths and have reverence for my sanctuary, I am the LORD. (v.2) "If you follow my decrees and are careful to obey my commands, (v.3) "I will send you rain in its season, and the ground will yield its crops and the trees of the field their fruit. (v. 4) "Your threshing will continue until grape harvest and the grape harvest will continue until planting, and you will eat all the food you want and live in safety in your land. (v.5) "I will grant peace in the land, and you will lie down and no one will make you afraid. (v.6) "I will remove savage beast from the land, and the sword will not pass through your country. You will pursue your enemies, and they will fall by the sword before you. (v.7) "Five of you will chase a hundred, and hundreds of you will chase ten thousand, and your enemies will fall by the sword before you. (v. 8) "I will look on you with favor and make you fruitful and increase your numbers, and I will keep my covenant with you. (v. 9) "You will still be eating last year's harvest when you will have to move it out to make room for the new. (v.10) "I will put my dwelling place among you, and I will not abhor you. (v.11) "I will walk among you and be your God, and you will be my people. (v. 12) "I am the LORD your God, who brought

you out of Egypt so that you would no longer be slaves to the Egyptians; I broke

the bars of your yoke and enabled you to walk with heads held high (v. 13)[39]

Challenges in Decision-Making

The increase incidence of climatic challenges offers yet another opportunity to apply our wits—wits that are increasingly becoming susceptible to futility.

When the nation is blessed, poor decision –making is less noticeable to the general public. It is during times of challenge that poor decision-making becomes seen as waste. Blessings are discussed in Leviticus in the Holy Bible. See Table 1.1.

TABLE 1.1

GOD'S INDICATORS/
Social Science Indicators
BLESSINGS

LEVITICUS 26	SOCIAL SCIENCE INDICATORS
Rain	Precipitation – Required Precipitation
produce,	Produce production - Self-sustaining
threshing shall last	Surplus Food Supplies – Stored Food
the full	Caloric Intake
safely	Rate of violent crime
peace in	Crime rate, political stability
none will make you afraid;	Security indicators
rid the land of evil beasts,	Death rate -animal attacks/threat, risk
sword will not go through	
your land.	Rate of violence in geographic borders
chase your enemies,	
and they shall fall	Rate of conquest of enemies/
	# of encounters
Five of you shall chase	
a hundred,	Ratio of military personnel/
	# of enemies routed
multiply you	Population Growth
confirm My covenant	Climate precipitation
old harvest	Food Stockpiles, Surplus
clear out the old because of new	Trade due to over supply
tabernacle among you, and	Revival, Rate of worship
I will walk among you	
and be your God,	Recognized as a Christian country
and you shall be My people.	
you should not be their slaves	No physical captivity, nor debt
you walk upright.	High standard of living

On the other hand, in times of want, a nation's poor decisions are more obvious because waste is un-masked by adversity. Adversity is presented as curses in Leviticus as can be seen in Table 1.2

TABLE 1.2

GOD'S INDICATORS/
Social Science Indicators
CURSES

LEVITICUS 26	SOCIAL SCIENCE INDICATORS
Wasting disease and fever	Rate of tuberculosis, Rate of HIV, etc.; Rate of fever
Weakened eyes	Rate of blindness
Sorrow of heart	Rate of emotional illness
Sow your seed in vain	Futility of effort; low yield
Enemies shall eat it	Foreign Rate of Consumption/displacement
Set my face against you	Low Rate of worship
Defeated by your enemies.	Rate of defeat in military events
Those who hate you shall reign over you	Enemy control over governance operations
flee when no one pursues you.	Rate of paranoia
break the pride of your power;	Loss of main industries
heavens like iron and your earth like bronze.	Environmental depletion
in vain	Low productivity rate
land shall not yield its produce,	Land designated unsuitable
nor fruit.	Low yield
wild beasts	Rate of animal hazard
destroy your livestock	Death & Disease rate in livestock
make you few in number	Population decline
highways shall be desolate.	Rate (decline) commercial trucking
sword against you	# of incidents of military engagements
send pestilence	Rate of pestilence/ severity/scope
delivered into the hand of the enemy.	# taken in captivity
supply of bread	Rate of food supply/scarcity
eat and not be satisfied.	Rate of caloric intake
shall eat the flesh of your sons,	
and you shall eat the flesh of your	
daughters	Rate of abortion
destroy your high places	Rate of destruction of geo symbols
carcasses on the lifeless forms	
of your idols	Causes of death
lay your cities waste	# of abandoned buildings, vacant space
sanctuaries to desolation,	# or abandoned churches/synagogue/mi
your enemies who dwell	Rate of crime
I will scatter you among the nations	Rate of out migration
a sword after you	Rate of violence
land shall be desolate and your	Rate of vacated space, housing
cities waste.	Rate of out migration from cities
land shall rest	# of years desolate
faintness into their hearts	Rate of heart attack
shaken leaf shall cause them to flee	Rate of perceived risk
flee as though fleeing from a sword	Rate of paranoia
fall when no one pursues	Rate of household injury; Rate of paranoia
stumble over one another	Rate of conflict
no power to stand before your enemies	Strategic vulnerability
perish among the nations	Absorption rates
land of your enemies shall eat you up.	Subjugation rate; subsistence
waste away in their iniquity in your enemies'	Rate of enslavement
fathers' iniquities,	Rate of inherited difficulty
	Life expectancy
they shall waste away.	Rate of desolation

On the occasion when the curses appear particularly acute is during war. Maladies referenced among the curses begin with the sixth item on the list and downward. Adversity is further exasperated by division within the nation. Such challenges occur when divisions exist between members of Congress and the President and or sharp divisions within the electorate.

So, to briefly recap, difficulties that have posed stumbling blocks in our nation:

> **Slavery** obscured Christian teaching with commercial self interest→Division within Church Community

> **Silence** on the part of the Church during the Holocaust→Separation of Church from the Jewish Community→ Fueled the growth of Secularization so that Church and State would not join forces in the United States against the Jewish population residing here.

These two (Slavery + Silence) fueled by secularization. As a consequence of slavery and silence, the fertile breeding ground of bitterness gave birth to multiculturalization and secularization.

Secularization in the Jewish Community emerged most visibly in the discipline of Social Work and with the Great Society programs in the sixties as a viable alternative to dependency on the part of churches given growing concern with the political involvement of the Black church making demands on the government.

Observation #1: Secularization → Increased government intervention via the provision of social services.

Observation #2: Secularism → Multiculturalism, domestically

Observation #3: Secularism → Multiculturalism, internationally

Observation #4: Secularism as official policy position, domestically→Secularism as official policy position, internationally.

And, the introduction of a multiculturalist perspective internationally presents unique challenges to national security.

Policy modeling given a secular mindset requires examining externals to create an outside-in system---changing the environment to improve the well-being of populations---corporately managed. This is in direct opposition to examining the internal (soul) conditions to create an inside out transformation that allows the individual to then change their external condition—changed hearts, changed minds and changed speech so that the environment becomes transformed, reflecting self-control via the Holy Spirit. Hence, self-governance results.

The absence of this self-control yields problematic disequilibrium.

We need to recognize the distinction that exists between God and the institution of the Church.

It is problematic that Church-state relations bog down normative questions with institution to institution comparison for the Gospel is shared to individuals who in aggregate constitute the Church. It is the individuals in aggregate that has direct influence the political system, not the institution of the church.

Yes, the scars of slavery and the Holocaust have obscured the truth about the God of Abraham, Isaac, and Jacob. No human being is guiltless here but Jesus Christ. It is He, Jesus, who is made unto us righteousness. He is the same God that became manifest in the Flesh, Adonai, Yeshua the Messiah, Christ Jesus. Many do not recognize who the Great Law Giver is.

A. W. Tozer describes the modern humanity's self-absorption as follows:

> One cannot long read the Scriptures sympathetically without noticing the radical disparity between the outlook of men of the Bible and that of modern men. We are today suffering from a secularized mentality. Where the sacred writers saw God, we see the laws of nature. Their world was alive and personal; ours is impersonal and dead. God ruled their world; ours is ruled by laws of nature and we are all removed from the presence of God.[40]

Then, Tozer poses and answers a critical question:

> And what are these laws of nature that have displaced God in the minds of millions? Law has two meanings. One is an external rule enforced by authority, such as the common rule against robbery and assault. The word is also used to denote the uniform way things act in the universe, but this second use of the word is erroneous. What we see in nature is simply the paths God's power and wisdom take through creation. Properly these are phenomena, not laws, but we call them laws by analogy with the arbitrary laws of society.[41]

> Science observes how the power of God operates, discovers a regular pattern somewhere and fixes it as a "law." The uniformity of God's activities in His creation enables the scientist to predict the course of natural phenomena. The trust worthiness of God's behavior in His world is the foundation of all scientific truth. Upon it the scientist rests his faith and from there he goes on to achieve great and useful things in such fields as those of navigation, chemistry, agriculture, and medical arts.[42]

Points of Access into the Policy Making Process

The Facts from a Biblical Perspective

1 - The degree to which a nation distances itself from God, the greater the incidence and severity of adverse condition to which the population will be put at risk due to faulty decision-making.

2 - The pattern of futility in response to those adverse conditions will render increased losses of life and property over time in the absence of repentance/revival.

3 - The policy problem that gets articulated as the consequence of the divinely permitted difficulty (either natural or unnatural) becomes a social agenda item defined in accordance with prevailing public policy assumptions that are secularized and primarily demographic.

4 - To the degree that a secularized response results, implementation will be susceptible to establishing a new or further strengthening an existing policy spiral.

5 - As time progresses, implementation will result in increased number of participants.

6 - Consequences of implementation will be recognizably locatable in one of four quadrants.

7 - To the degree that the problem may be defined in response to a perceived infringement of one demographic group over another, the implementation spiral will become entrenched.

FIGURE 2.1

Big Picture

Public Policy Cycle

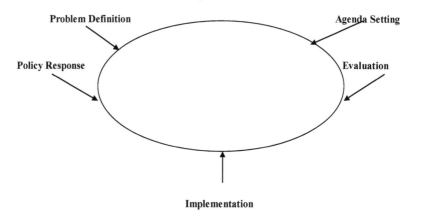

The typical kinds of questions of a political nature the public policy analyst encounters are listed below. And, these questions coincide with the processes associated with the making and execution of public policy. The public policy-making process has the following stage as seen in the figure below.   Whether in times of feast or famine, a discernible pattern to policymaking stages exists. See Table 2.1

TABLE 2.1
PUBLIC POLICY PROCESS STAGES

	HOGWOOD & GUNN[43]	DUNN[44]
STAGE 1	Deciding to decide (Issue Search and Agenda Setting)	Problem Structuring
STAGE 2	Deciding how to decide (Issue Filtration)	---
STAGE 3	Issue Definition	Policy Problems
STAGE 4	Forecasting	Forecasting
STAGE 5	Setting Objectives and Priorities	Policy Alternatives
STAGE 6	Optional Analysis (Routes to achieving a Given policy decision)	Recommendations
STAGE 7	Policy Implementation Monitoring and Control	Policy Actions Monitoring
STAGE 8	Evaluation and Review	Policy Outcomes Evaluation
STAGE 9	Policy Maintenance Succession or Termination	Policy Performance Practical Inference Policy Problem

TABLE 2.1 presents the major stages associated with public policy and the types of inquiry that may accompany each stage. The policy process consists of agenda setting, policy and program formulation and legitimization, program implementation, and evaluation. With each of these stages there are evaluative activities that are pursued. Beginning with agenda setting, the idea is to identify the status of the country based upon captured information on census, business, exchange, and other concerns that summarize aspects of quality of life. The goal is a kind of social auditing to determine current status, to compare this with previous status, and ultimately to make some determination about the acceptability of where we are with regard to the concerns that led to the capture of that information. In its simple form, detection of social conditions may mean a mere review of social indicators. In a strategic approach, it will mean the establishment of a

threshold of acceptable or unacceptable status to which those social indicators are to be compared. To complete this portion of the picture, there should be a determination of demand and/or degree of coverage of policy with regard to populations that fall below an established threshold.

Problem Definition

The biblically informed can respond in a God–honoring fashion.

To do so, the following societal audit questions deserve consideration. How is your nation in treating the aliens, widows, and orphans, the most vulnerable of the population? What is the official posture of your nation with regard to these groups? Is the official posture actually evident by action? Since these groups tend to be socially vulnerable --a condition recognized as worthy of concern in Holy Scripture -the vulnerable are a good barometer of societal conditions.

The next question is concerning potential stakeholders. Have stakeholders acknowledged known wrong doings among themselves, in their own organizations; and, have they done the corrective actions needed to avoid repeat offense? In other words, have these stakeholders humbled themselves before God, repented, and implemented the change(s) required in their own individual organizations? If they have, and intend to seek God's guidance on every aspect of their operations and the suggestion offered for the nation, then the emerging country will have maximum likelihood of national transformation.

Finally, where does the country stand with regard to international issues, in particular regarding the sovereignty of Israel? This question is not without consequence. Israel is important to God.

Care should be given to determine just how progress should be measured, especially in response to key policy arguments?

The question might be asked, "What does this mean in terms of the secular environment; biblically framed initiatives; multiculturalism; invasion of other gods; policy agendas in prodigal societies." The answer is societal estimations and declared problem definition that proceeds without benefit of the decision-making that begins with right acknowledgement of God possesses within the decision seeds of futility. The challenge is to explore the implications of strategic decision-making in the direction of governance that has its point of departure the acknowledgement of God to consider an alternative approach to assessing public policy issues that incorporates the tools needed for testing the truthfulness of explanation upon which future action may rest. We offer a biblically informed approach to public policy decision making so that God may be rightly acknowledge in the making of decisions of state.

In summary to this point, the situation is this:

GOD'S INTERVENTION NOT EASILY SEEN BECAUSE:

---Church remained divided on issue of Slavery. Not able to come to a consensus on what would constitute the right thing to do despite the fact they nevertheless purported to worship the same God. God is not the author of confusion. So, what fueled this division was self interest. Self interest on the part of Southern slave owners even though ownership of slaves was a financially unfruitful venture. And, self interest on the part of northerners who did not own slaves but preferred to intellectualize their description of God's attributes as a means of avoidance of His commands[45]

---Church world-wide failed Jews. Only lone voices like that of Dietrich Bonhoeffer[46] spoke out against the atrocities because the established church conformed to the Nazi political order.[47]

Even though it is in Christ that we live and move and have our being,

God's intervention is further obscured because a few high pitched notions that have since followed.

---Separation of Church and State arguments fervently presented as if the institution of the Church were God, Himself. Human failings plus a desire to make Attempting to mold God into our own image reduced arguments to that which ignored the God's ownership of all authority, including that of government. [48]

---Jewish social activists reinforced secularization and were instrumental in the development of social policies and programs that did not reinforce family but help to dismantle it.[49]

---Jewish intellectuals endorsed the secularized social agenda because of the fear of the possible consequences of state church alliances like that which occurred in Hitler's Germany.[50]

---U.S. Government in response to Civil Rights activity picks up policies and programs that are rooted in Secular agenda [51]

---Secular Jews do not consider Israel of spiritual value because they are hard hearted against God—[52]

---Secular social policies and programs multiplied domestically and then spread internationally with internationalized interest groups---environmentalism/paganism as the book of Romans predicts with the worship of the creature rather than the Creator. [53]

As a consequence of all of the above,

---Social conflict has existed between Ethnic Jews and the Church[54]

---Social distance exists between Ethnic Jews and Messianic Jews[55]

---Social distance exists between Secular Jews and Fundamentalist Christians[56]

---Social distance exists between Pagans and non-secular Jews and Christians[57]

---Social distance exists between nations and the alliance of the United States with the nation of Israel [58]

---Spiritual distance exists between the lost and God[59].

And, as a final consequence:

---Since the world is angry with God, the world rejects what God loves. This is an example of Cain and Abel replayed.[60]

---Charges of exclusivity are rendered by secularists in an attempt to undermine Judeo-Christian, biblical notions[61]

---And, most importantly, moral clarity is lost because God is not acknowledged

What the comparison of accounts of the public policy process typically omits are the elements that dynamically emerge from decision making that takes place in the affairs of state. Those elements consist of Competing Problem Definition; Non-Problem or Disparately Problematic Situations; and, Problem Distancing yielding the Policy Implementation Spiral all adding up to futility of effort in governance. Explored in the next chapter are the consequences of failed acknowledgment of God. I call those adverse consequences *Policy Spirals.*

ACTION POINT

A series of steps remain associated with the logic of written argument. The following consists of a condensed form of what could be encountered from any rhetoric text on the mechanics of building an argument. What I am about to describe represents a short composite gleaned from the reading of a number of logic and rhetoric texts. A. M. Tibbetts, *The Strategies of Rhetoric* (Tibbetts 1969) and M. Scriven, *Reasoning* (Scriven 1976) lead my list as being particularly insightful and well-deserving of special mention. Indeed, Tibbetts maintains that the exchange of ideas in the form of argument serve as a foundation for the pursuit of Truth. Both of the above mentioned authors stress understanding the architectural structure of written argument. [62]

Well, having digested this information for you, I recommend that you review the outline of steps associated with the presence of any written argument. The following list comes from my limited access document entitled, *Analytical Bridge for the Literary Mind* (McDonald 2006).

These steps can help you build and critique argument:

Step 1 Clarification of Argument by specifying the meaning of the argument and its component parts

This includes specifying the meaning of terms, phrases, suggestions, corresponding implications, etc.

Step 2 Identification of stated and unstated conclusions associated with the argument

Look for "because" cues and the sequences offered as a chain.

Step 3 Assessment of the structure of the argument

This requires the identification of operative imagery for the prevailing argument. Identify the presumed relation between premises and conclusions by isolating parts of the argument. Then, determine what supports exist for the conclusions. I suggest you draw a picture or diagram if need be to map out the argument as a part of your review.

Step 4 Identification of missing or otherwise unstated premises

Perhaps the most challenging portion of the exercise, you must recognize the arguer's assumptions; the assumptions seen as the necessary conditions for the argument; the assumptions associated with the strongest claims of the argument.

Step 5 Critique of the given premises

This step requires the examination of inferences in a sequence so that if the argument offered suggests that   B comes as a consequence of A, you should check to see if adequate support exists for that inference.

Step 6 Critique of the unstated (missing) premises

 If the argument given suggests: A--->B---->D, you should identify the missing C that would be appropriate for the sequence and Why?

Step 7 Critique of inferences

What counter examples exist? This requires using your "sanctified" imagination to explore the same issue but do so by applying the mind of Christ to the issue. Do all A's consist of B's or do cases of A's exist that do not belong to the category of "not B's." This counter example idea may be applied to definition, inference, interpretation, analysis, and imagery.

Step 8   Introduction of relevant arguments otherwise omitted from discussion

Contrasts emerge when a biblical worldview envelops serious thought about a policy issue. Discuss the consequences of omission associated with the premises that accompany secular discussions of your topic. And, then discuss the reshaping of options that comes with right application of the biblical worldview, specifying what this means for the conclusions presented in the argument.

Step 9 Summative evaluation of the overall argument

Give supportable criticism—that for which credible evidence emerges, such that even those who do not share our biblical understanding can no longer ignore the truthfulness of our claim, eliminating the possibility to attribute your stated results to something other than the concrete logic/evidence you have presented.

CHAPTER THREE

Acknowledging God in Developing Policy Agendas in

Prodigal Society

"For although they knew God, they neither glorified him as God nor gave thanks to him, but their thinking became futile and their foolish hearts were darkened. Although they claimed to be wise, they became fools and exchanged the glory of the immortal God for images made to look like mortal man and birds and animals and reptiles."[63]

Recap

1. Slavery and the Holocaust as political realities have had lasting consequences. Slavery obscured Christian teaching with commercial self-interest→Division within Church Community
2. Holocaust Silence on the part of the Church →Separation of Church from the Jewish Community→ Fueled the growth of Secularization as a preventive measure so that Church and State would not join forces against the Jewish population residing in the United States as had happened been the case in Hitler's Germany.
3. The seeds of two events: Pre-Civil War Slavery in the United States + Holocaust Silence continue to fuel secularization, with reinforced recollection of both events providing breeding ground for bitterness that undergirds secularization.
4. Secularization in the Jewish community surfaced through the applied study of social work for the Great Society policies and programs in the sixties, then seen as a viable option to dependency on the part of churches, and marking the growing concern with the political involvement of the Black church making demands on the government.

5. The merger of a political agenda with that of socio-dynamics of the church in Black communities as being the only recognizable organizational hierarchy within the *community led to prominent platforms for religious oratory applied to social* issues, making ripe the influx of social theology geared for the hearing of those who perceive themselves as "down-trodden."

So, *in essence,*

Secularization → Increased government intervention via the provision of social services

Secularism → Multiculturalism, *domestically*

Secularism → Multiculturalism, *internationally*

Secularism as official policy position, domestically→Secularism as official policy position, *internationally*

What makes the above especially problematic is that *this introduction of multi-cultural perspective internationally serves to undermine our national security*.

It is also imperative that we face the fact that "Faith Based" strategies exhibit the propensity to become multicultural rather than a deliverance intervention strategy.

Secular approaches to policy development come from a mindset that examines externals to create an outside-in system---changing the environment to improve the well-being of populations---populations to be corporately managed. This is in direct opposition to taking a biblically informed approach, one that takes into account the internal (soul) conditions of individuals in the aggregate, supporting conditions that permit an inside out transformation. The inside-out approach that allows the individuals to experience internal transformation results in those same individuals altering their own behavior in a way that then changes their external condition. Changed hearts result in changed minds and changed speech as well as action so that the environment becomes transformed. Individuals exercise self-control via the Holy Spirit and hence are then equipped to exercise self-governance. The absence of this self-control yields problematic disequilibrium.

CAUTION required here:

It is possible to exercise reform, "outside-in," however, the results will not be self-sustaining. Also, with reform comes greater restriction of personal liberty. And, with the absence of vigilant "reformers", strides may quickly fall away opening up the individual and the aggregate of individuals that constitute a nation to the increased severity of problem similar to the phenomenon described in Luke11: 24-26. That passage says, *"When an evil spirit comes out of a man, it goes through arid places seeking rest and does not find it. Then it says, 'I will return to the house I left' When it arrives, it finds the house swept clean and put in order. Then it goes ad takes seven other spirits more wicked than itself, and they go in and live there. And the final condition of that man is worse than the first."*

In other words, to clean one's house [self effort associated with one's life as an individual, as well as well meaning effort to clean up individuals in the aggregate as a nation], does not guarantee that the strides made will stay that way. Vacuums not only get filled, but get filled with that which is much worse. This by the way is why "democracy," that is the status of "constitutional republic" may not be imposed nor transferred successfully on to a society that lacks right relationship with God of the Holy Bible. Jesus Christ Himself is quite definitive about the alignment of sides in this life. He says in Luke 11:23,

> *"He who is not with me is against me, and he who does not gather with me, scatters."*[64]

He also says in John 15:5,

> *"I am the vine; you are the branches. Whoever abides in me and I in him, he it is that bears much fruit, for apart from me you can do nothing."*[65]

Propositions Pertaining to God-Honoring Governance

The propositions discussed in the remainder of this chapter seek to identify the relation of factors that undermine the possibility of success for policy initiatives to be addressed by the Daniels and Josephs of our age, Saints called to governance. Propositions follow from three themes: (1) **problem definition, (2) problems that are**

disparately problematic, and (3) problem distancing due to policy implementation spirals. All apply to both the domestic and the international arena.

- The greater the degree to which a nation distances itself from God, the greater the incidence and severity of adverse condition to which the population will be put at risk due to inappropriate decision-making. [*Romans 1:24*]
- In the absence of moral clarity, a pattern of futility in response to those adverse conditions will render increased losses of life and property over time in the absence of repentance/revival. [*Romans 1:28*]
- The policy issue [*Leviticus 26:14-39*] that comes as the consequence of the divinely permitted difficulty (either natural or manmade) then becomes a social agenda item defined in accordance with prevailing public policy assumptions that are secularized and primarily demographic.
- To the degree that a secularized response results, implementation will be susceptible to establishing new or further strengthening existing policy spirals. [*Ecclesiastes 2:11*]
- As time progresses, implementation will result in increased number of participants. [*See 1 Kings 11:3, the example taken from the life of King Solomon who pursued marriages as mergers for purposes of diplomacy/foreign relations*]
- Consequences of implementation will be recognizably locatable on the accuracy of problem definition and appropriate implementation of response. [*God honoring discernment appropriates correct definition and then strategy for achievement, justice. An example can be seen in the early reign of King Solomon, 1 Kings 3:16-28*]
- To the degree that the problem may be defined in response to a perceived infringement of one demographic group over another, the implementation spiral will become entrenched. [*An example may be seen in 2 Samuel 10:2-9*]

Let us explore now how to receive deliverance from the pattern of futility that characterizes current patterns of governance.

As you are no doubt aware by now, it is my contention that the sovereignty of our nation rests squarely upon our right recognition of the God of the Holy Bible as Sovereign of the universe. Without right recognition of Jesus Christ among His professed followers, there is no assurance that Truth or justice will prevail within corridors of power.

In the absence of right acknowledgment of God of Holy Bible, we collectively cease to operate in our right mind as a nation. What emerges on the airway, in the large metropolis, and in the hamlet, is just so much empty expression, especially as people judge themselves and others by themselves.

Socio-political voices would have us limit our review of candidates for elections to that of the economic landscape—an ownership realm that is suggestive for sure. But, please don't miss the BIG PICTURE HERE. Any relevance economic indicators have in our selection processes should have import only because of God. It is not humanity but God Himself that grants ability to make wealth. Nor, should we fall into the trap of thinking that the accumulation of wealth is somehow to be seen as a solid indicator of "right" relationship with God. The fact is that the enemy of our souls can be permitted to lavish wealth in our direction accompanied by "leanness of soul" as a judgment from God. No, Saints, ours is a narrow road that requires relationship with Jesus Christ to maintain right bearings independent of circumstance.

It is also important to remember that the God of the Bible has given His people a much higher standard by which to discern appropriate action. That guidance by the Holy Spirit is cultivated by the reading of HIS Word, the Holy Bible.

<u>Unfortunately, what makes our current condition even more precarious is the fact that as a nation we have a history of making money off of broken systems.</u>

Here is what I mean.

Sin generates spending beyond our means as persons and as institutions. That which is not of God drives the search for purchasable goods and services as a means of shoring up or otherwise distracting our attention from our true state. Purchase to "improve quality of life" desensitizes us as a population to the fact that we are trying to live this life without God. As I mentioned in an earlier entry, Sin costs! And, the money we personally and collectively spend beyond our real needs is used to minimize the short-term discomforts associated with our distance from God.

God has a different plan for His people. His Word says, "Where the Spirit of the Lord is there is liberty." Liberty costs, too, in covenant commitment.

The question is, *"Are we really willing to pay the cost?"*
Now, prayerfully, let's take another look, a good look, at each of those commands from God. And, let's identify what violation looks like and what the implications are for our present age.

The Ten Commandments

1. I AM the LORD your God, who brought you out of Egypt, out of the land of slavery, you shall have no other gods before me.

Violation of Commandment #1 comes from the willingness to so reverence prominence and possessions; many times, we secure these by virtue of our labor plus the making of decisions characteristic of "people pleasing" to the neglect of God given responsibilities. We each must take a prayerful inventory of what we do on a daily basis. We should start the day with God so that He can order our steps, we should end the day with accountability to God for how we spent the time He has given us this day. This would improve governance of our individual households. It would also improve governance of our nation.

2. You shall not make for yourself an idol in the form of anything in heaven above or on the earth beneath or in the water below. You shall not bow down to them or worship them; for I, the LORD your God, am a jealous God, punishing the children for the sin of the fathers to the third and fourth generation of those who hate me, but showing love unto a thousand generation of those who love Me and keep My Commandments.

There is much that can be said about this command. But, for now let's discuss what *captivates* our attention because that is in effect what an idol is. What do we put most of our energy into? What do we fear losing the most? What values do we demonstrate (not just say) motivates how we approach each day? My Dad who was a wonderful, spirit-filled Christian man of God, would say to me, *"Livvy,* it's not what people say that tells you who they are. It's what they do." That sage insight from my earthly Dad has carried me a long way in this life. It did so, not just because of the meaningfulness of what he said. It did so, because I saw who he was with every move he made. I saw Christ Jesus in the loving compassion and generosity of my Dad. I saw the contrary in many others. And, what we expose our children to is what gets passed down from generation to generation.

3. You shall not misuse the name of the LORD your God, for the LORD will not hold anyone guiltless who misuses His name.

I once thought that the misuse of the Name of the LORD was limited to cursing, vulgar slinging of "Jesus" impulsively or emotively without one care in the world about Who He is or the problem of blasphemy. It has come to my attention late in life that taking the Name of the LORD in vain includes our purporting to be Christ followers, yet denying Who He is by the decisions we make (decisions like supporting those individuals or ideologies that counter what God says in His written word, the Holy Bible) and acting contrary to what God would have us do. In other words, our actions can be an expression of taking the Name of the LORD in vain, especially if those actions are exhibited to others who will see what we "Christians" do that is not Christ-like, and thus becomes an obstacle to salvation.

4. Observe the Sabbath day by keeping it holy, as the LORD your God has commanded you. Six days you shall labor and do all your work, but the seventh day is a Sabbath to the LORD your God. On it you shall not do any work, neither you, nor your son or daughter, nor your manservant or maidservant, or your ox, your donkey or any of your animals, not the alien within your gates, so that your manservant and maidservant may rest, as you do. Remember that you were slaves

in Egypt and that the LORD your God brought you out of there with a mighty hand and an outstretched arm. Therefore the LORD your God has commanded you to observe the Sabbath.

There is much that can be said here, too. But, suffice it to say that one day in seven we need to rest in the Lord, be especially mindful of Him and worship Him. We need to Remember Him. And, by "Remember Him" I am not just suggesting thinking about Him although, of course, that is what we are doing. By "Remembering Him" I am suggesting that we "Re-Member Him" meaning that we who are each Members of His Body need to re-assemble ourselves as a full expression of Who He is in Him at least one day in Seven. So, not only are we to recollect our mind, body, and spirit in alignment with Who God is privately, we are to manifest collectively Who He is in our congregational worship of Him.

Recently, a pastor whose church was the site of one of our National Day of Prayer locations said, "The World is made up of broken relationships. If you turn on any of the talk shows, all they are about is broken relationships. The answer is here in 1John. We need right relationship with Jesus Christ. If we are right with Him, we will walk in the light as God is in the Light. Right relationship with God makes possible right relationship with others." To this, I say Amen. Relationships must be protected and nurtured, especially with God. I find myself having to repent and reconnect, repent and reconnect with Jesus, for as times progress, the offenses are on the rise. Many can be recurring from a familiar source. Can you imagine how much more productive our nation would be if we did not have the mindset of needing to escape our circumstances but become stronger and better because of them? God grants grace. Amen! I say, Hallelujah for the human sanctification agents that give us a workout so that we become strong in this life and simultaneously strengthen our longing for heaven. Amen!

5. Honor your father and your mother, as the LORD your God has commanded you, so that you may live long and that it may go well with you in the land that the LORD your God is giving you.

Bible teachers are quick to point out that this is the only Commandment of the ten that comes with a promise. This means that independent of the caliber of person your parents are, they are your parents. God did not make a mistake with giving you those parents even if they are the most horrendous persons that have ever breathed. We are to honor them because God says so. If we do, He will give us the grace to live in freedom from whatever oppression the enemy of our souls intends. This is a good conversation to consider as we and our parents age. A Google site lists the following definitions for honor:

> --. Esteem due or paid to worth; high estimation; respect; consideration; reverence; veneration; manifestation of respect or reverence.
> --. That which rightfully attracts esteem, respect, or consideration; self-respect; dignity; courage; fidelity; especially, excellence of character; high moral worth; virtue; nobleness; specif., in men, integrity; uprightness; trustworthiness; in women, purity; chastity.
> --. A nice sense of what is right, just, and true, with course of life correspondent thereto; strict conformity to the duty imposed by conscience, position, or privilege.
> --. That to which esteem or consideration is paid; distinguished position; high rank.
> --. Fame; reputation; credit
> --. A token of esteem paid to worth; a mark of respect; a ceremonial sign of consideration; as, he wore an honor on his breast; military honors; civil honors.
> --. A cause of respect and fame; a glory; an Excellency; an ornament; as, he is an honor to his nation.
> --. A title applied to the holders of certain honorable civil offices, or to persons of rank; as, His Honor the Mayor. See Note under Honorable....etc[66]

In conclusion, we honor God when we honor what He wants us to honor. That should be sufficient reason to do so. Can you imagine the difference in health we would experience if we were not constantly haunted by *"Why?"* questions with regard to parents and loved ones? Pharmaceutical companies would have to rethink their money making products.

6. You shall not murder.

This translation is a good one as so many use the term "kill" rather than "murder." "Murder" is the right translation. We are to recognize that God does not endorse "Murder," unlawful killing of one human by another, especially with premeditated malice according to legal dictionaries. And, as Christians, the definition includes "hatred" as in those incidences when we do hate, we are "murderers in our hearts." Can you imagine how much more efficiently we would operate if we didn't have to go out of our way to avoid certain folks because we "hate" them. More importantly, can you imagine how many inventors, discoverers of medical break-through, technological innovators have been murdered via abortion. Someone who God gave the ability to provide a cure for cancer may have already been dismembered in his mother's womb. A moral outrage for sure! *And,* economic setback!

7. You shall not commit adultery.

Let's look at this word, "adultery." The New Webster Dictionary defines it as unlicensed intercourse, infidelity, cuckoldry, extramarital affair; then says see fornication. A better definition may be found in the Webster Unabridged that says,

   "1.violation of the marriage bed; sexual intercourse between a married man and a woman not his wife, or between a married woman and a man, hot her husband. Adulterer is a common legal ground for divorce. 2. in Scripture, all manner of lewdness or unchastity; also, idolatry or apostasy. And, interestingly enough, Webster gives a third definition which is, "in ecclesiastical affairs, the intrusion of a person into a bishopric during the life of the bishop."

   At the very root of the word, "adultery," is implied the word, "adulterate." To adulterate is to "debase" with a foreign mixture. To be "adulterous" is to be spurious and corrupt.
We are not to be spurious or corrupt.

We are to keep our God ordained covenant.

Just a special note here: In my reading of late, I have found an interesting set of facts that I will interpret in this way because I believe it to be the truth. Economically, God has allowed our financial situation to plummet to the point that it is now economically too expensive to divorce. One household is cheaper than two. Think about it. "It's cheaper to keep her," is even more true today! Hallelujah! Amen!

8. You shall not steal.

With the definition of the word, "steal" we understand that we are not to:
take or appropriate (another's property, ideas, etc.) without permission, dishonestly, or unlawfully, especially in a secret or surreptitious manner.
Webster says the word is synonymous with pilfer, purloin, plunder, rob, filch, thieve, swindle, and rifle. We are not to do this. If we are in right relationship with Jesus, He can give us the moral clarity that leads to invention and prosperity using the work of our own hands. Without inventiveness--a gift from God--there is no creative or unique contribution to be made for the benefit of ourselves or our society.

9. You shall not give false testimony against your neighbor.
We are not to lie about anyone. We are to tell the Truth in Love.

10. You shall not covet your neighbor's wife. You shall not set your desire on your neighbor's house or, his manservant or maidservant, his ox or donkey, or anything that belongs to your neighbor.

We are not to be envious of what others have. Folks would be free to fear that their possessions will be ransacked or otherwise taken away.

We know that these Ten Commandments will not save us. Nor, can we keep them in our own strength. They served a useful purpose for our salvation in that we realize that God's standards are higher than man's. We recognize that we fail, we sin, meaning we fall short of the glory of God. And, that's why we cry out to the only one who can save us, Christ Jesus Our Lord. Through Him, God has made a provision for us so that those Commandments can be kept. What God had done is give us His Son, Christ Jesus, to live His life through us. We are His body. May the Holy Spirit not be grieved but become so comfortable in us that He guide all of our actions in this life.

Saints, what makes the World uncomfortable is the convicting presence of God's Holy Spirit that comes with the display of those Ten Commandments. To those who take offense, we invite you to a higher life, a life in relationship with Jesus. "Come, let us reason together," says the Lord. Though your sins, your acts that serve only to further distance yourself from Me, be the color of scarlet--a bright, big, red STOP LIGHT that is troubling and terribly inconvenient because it reminds you from of where you have plunged, let Me make those sins white as new fallen snow. You can be saved from those self-destructive patterns of life you have grown accustomed to. Just ask for forgiveness, and accept the provision I have made for you, says the Lord. Accept Christ Jesus into your life. Say, "Come into my life, Lord Jesus!"

ACTION POINT

Consider:

Proverbs 1:29-2:1-5 says:

> *Since they hated knowledge and did not choose to fear the LORD, Since they would not accept my advice and spurned my rebuke, they will eat the fruit of their ways and be filled with the fruit of their schemes.*
>
> *For the waywardness of the simple will kill them, and the complacency of fools will destroy them; but whoever listens to me will live in safety and be at ease, without fear of harm.*
>
> *My son, if you accept my words and store up my commands within you, turning your ear to wisdom and applying your heart to understanding, and if you call out for insight and cry aloud for understanding, and if you look for it as for silver and search for it*

> *as for hidden treasure, then you will understand the fear of the*
> *LORD and find the knowledge of God.*

Unfortunately, as things currently stand, Proverbs 24:30-34 more accurately describes
where we are today:
That proverb says,

> *I went past the field of the sluggard, past the vineyard of the man*
> *who lacks judgment; thorns had come up everywhere, the ground*
> *was covered with weeds, and the wall was in ruins.*

> *I applied my heart to what I observed and learned a lesson from*
> *what I saw: a little sleep, a little slumber, a little folding of the*
> *hands to rest---and poverty will come on you like a bandit and*
> *scarcity like an armed man.*

It is important to recognize the distinction that exists between God and the institution
of the Church. It is problematic that Church-state relations bog down normative
questions by way of "institution to institution" comparison. We must remind ourselves
that the Gospel is shared to individuals who in aggregate constitute the Church. It is
those individuals in aggregate, collectively, that have direct influence the political
system, quality and vigilance of governance, and not the institution of the church. Yes,
the scars of slavery and the Holocaust have obscured the truth about the God of Abraham,
Isaac, and Jacob. No human being is guiltless here but Jesus Christ. It is He, Jesus, who
is made unto us righteousness. He is the same God that became manifest in the flesh,
Adonai, Yeshua the Messiah, Christ Jesus. Many do not recognize the Great Law Giver.
Modern humanity's self-absorption obstructs vision.

Having expressed that thought, I must quickly speak to the role of pastors, a role
that must remain clear. I believe the following to be imperative elements to our correct
understanding:
1. The continued sovereignty of the United States remains directly linked to the degree
to which the Bible Believing Church rightly acknowledges the sovereignty of God and
operates according to the Word of God, the Holy Bible.

2. The founders of the United States were effective because of their basic understanding

of the foundational Truth that the establishment of a great nation must rest securely upon the Holy Bible, a sentiment echoed even as recently as the nineteen eighties in this country by President Reagan when in 1983 he wrote a proclamation that 1983 was The Year of the Bible.

3. The result of right recognition of the need for the adherence to the Holy Bible, the thorough reading of it even to the point of re-writing paraphrase portions [as Jefferson did] resulted in greater and greater understanding of its contents and translated into a keen understanding and clarity of thought required to establish this nation.

4. The founders tapped into the mind of Christ as revealed in the Holy Bible and the result was Providential guidance that led to the writing of the Declaration of independence and (ultimately) the Constitution of the United States.

5. It is imperative that we return to the Holy Bible as the guiding document for our lives individually and collectively as followers of Christ Jesus. [This is the humbling required by 2 Chronicles 7:14, it is not simply the getting on our knees and praying, it is prayerfully reading God's Word, understanding what God wants us to do, and then doing it rather than going our own way prescribing our own version of what constitutes right and wrong. Such error results in quagmire and death spiritually and physically to ourselves and others as seen with the most recent rumblings of congregational error.

6. A return to the reading and application of the Holy Bible as the inerrant Word of God is imperative if this nation is to survive because only then will God-given reason return to this country, to citizenry.

7. If the population begins to acknowledge the God of the Bible--starting with the churches (because if the churches get it right, their congregations will get it right and read the Bible for guidance in decision-making)--then the general population will be able to see a difference between Egypt and Goshen.

8. As it stands now, with the full range from lukewarm to that of outrageously wrong doctrine, the world won't (can't) see any difference between the church and the world.

9. That is why the most patriotic thing a citizen of the United States can do is study the Holy Bible, because in it is life, and by it all of God's servants are warned, given divinely inspired discernment needed to make right choices in this world and to be saved through the acceptance of Christ Jesus for the next.

10. Because of the great fractures within the body of Christ across ethnic, racial, denominational, political, and theological lines, there must be return to what God says. It is the only way to restoration collectively to right place as members of His Body.

11. Further, it is imperative that Pastors be schooled on the relationship between the Holy Bible, the Declaration of Independence and the U.S. Constitution, to move beyond the "man-centered" focus on founders, men who were just as fallen as we are, to a focus on the Creator of the universe, the Sovereign that raises up and brings down nations.

12. Pastors need to know the relevance of Bible scriptures to the governance of our nation.

13. Pastors need to return not merely to the founders as their end point, but rather and most sincerely to the Biblical Foundation upon which the founders of this nation looked.

14. Rightly taught, a look at history will take into account God's use of the founders in His plans, in which case the founders are a good reference point for discussion. But, understand this. Any failure to go a step further, to look beyond the founders will mean receipt of an history lesson limited to history of men rather **HIS story**, which is the "real" story, THE story of God intervening in the affairs of men.

15. Pastors must be revived, returning to their first Love as revealed to them in the Holy Bible, saying what God says from cover to cover of the Holy Bible, showing its

relevance and application, so that their congregants will read the Bible for themselves with understanding, knowing what should be done,   as well as what should not be done or tolerated.

16.   Unless the dots are connected between the Holy Bible and the notion of "self-governance" which only comes by way of "self control," a gift of the Holy Spirit, any strides made now will be superficial, failing to stop the erosion of our nation's character.

17. As we know from God's Word, the Holy Spirit calls to memory at the right time what the Christian has read in the Holy Bible. If the Christian does not read the Bible, there is nothing to call to memory.

18. Since there are so many counterfeit spirits and false "christs" active in our world, God warns us to test all ideas and spirits on the basis of what is written in the Holy Bible.
19. When what one hears does not line up with the Holy Bible, the notion should be rejected. That is called *discernment*. The Holy Bible is the litmus test for all ideas and arguments!

20. In no way should we as Christ followers stand in awe of the founders of the nation as they were mere mortals, *too*. [The error is easy to make because of the divinely influenced writing.] Awe must be reserved for God!   Not God *And...*

21.   Because of the emotional makeup of patriotic fervor, such a displacement can also happen. We must at all times remember that this nation has been great because it was dedicated at its inception to our GREAT GOD! And, it was and is only possible because of His great hand guiding us.

22. We MUST look for God's guidance in practical terms just as the founders did. It is our generation's turn to apply the Holy Bible to governance of our lives for our nation.[67]

CHAPTER FOUR

Acknowledging God vs. Missing the Mark: The Policy Spiral

"Make a tree good and the fruit will be good. Make a tree bad and the fruit will be bad. For a tree is recognized by its fruit."[68] Matthew 12:33, Holy Bible

This chapter discusses God and Us, explaining the dynamics of public policy genealogy, the case of problem incongruence and the path of exodus from the whirlwind of policy implementation spirals. But, first, let us review what it is we seek to correct.

Revisiting the Pattern of Futility Yielding Policy Spirals

--The solution to the declared problem will be more reflective of the problem's original (biblically sound) definition at the inception of a public policy than over time.

--As time progresses, the numbers of actors involved in the process of problem resolution increase.

--As time progresses, the diversity of actors involved in the process of problem resolution increase.

--Actor diversity yields problem redefinition.

--With diversity, problem definition administratively changes.

--The original problem appears more complex with privatization.

--The original problem appears more complex due to expert status.

--Incorrect problem definition yields the public policy spiral.

Yes. We have long understood that the whole process of understanding of anything comes from a myriad of strategic decisions. There is the decision to observe phenomena; the decision to accept any one of a variety of plausible explanations; the decision to select a specific test as a way of determining the credibility of an explanation; the decision to accept a particular interpretation of the result; the decision to terminate inquiry. Even with all of those decisions in mind, it is possible to fail to discover. Exposure to the scientific method early in our academic and professional careers has pounded into our psyche the composite parts of discovery: observation, explanation, testing, analysis, and new observation with the idea that that the process will go indefinitely.

Even though we are familiar with the stated process, the idea of knowing entails notions greater than what remains captured above. Knowing involves the activities of observing a phenomenon; explaining why the phenomenon exists; and then testing the explanation. Questions of causality must invariably kick in if we are rational human beings. This is problematic in the postmodern age where questions of causality lead ultimately to questions of first cause which, of course, is God. In scholarly circles, "how to see" is rarely if ever discussed within the traditional context of research method classes, especially those directed toward public policy and evaluation. Component parts of discovery in the construction of theory that are typically not discussed are the point of focus for this treatise because analogy is vital to the discovery process---its use and the avoidance of its abuse; types of explanatory imagery; and , consequences for different analogy and format of explanation. The above being a critical element due to our need for theory –driven evaluation of policymaking and programmatic activity.

From the social sciences, we know that the process of observing can be as fundamental as exploring one's on environment or as sophisticated as employment of analogy. Seeing is further complicated by the presence of obstacles that may impede one's clarity of vision when seeking *"to know"*. This means the exploration of such elements as the structure of attention and amount of detectable change in points of focus. All of this is, of course, related to issues and changing outcome, the appropriate question being---to what degree is there a difference in outcome that is evidentially a consequence of policy action. Other curiosities found in literature may pertain to such concepts as decision burden, information, and either temporal or spatial configuration patterns of policy implementation activity.

Decoding the Pattern of Futility: Thought Processes of Cain

What is Derivative Thought?

Derivative thought starts from a fragmented element of the truth-fractured by distance from God and moves builds plans based upon that fractured view.[7] Derivative thought is what results in government policy spirals. Because the solutions strategies miss the mark in the first place, the results are at best a temporarily beneficial, contradictory, and unstable for the society to move forward. This problem is keen in the developed world and is the primary obstacle to nation building in the less developed world.

The problem of derivative thought is the first stage toward wicked reasoning. Wicked reasoning is an irrationality that serves to twist aspects of reality into conformity with our base nature. The twisting serves like wicker. The twists are capsulated renditions of fragmented truths that lead to circular reasoning. Truth prevails but not in a form readily understandable to point of being beneficial because of the distorted perceptions that animosity toward God yields.

Returning again to the Genesis 4 account, we find Cain, angered at God's unwillingness to accept what Cain offered resulted in Cain's killing of his brother, Abel. The problem was that Cain offered to God what he deemed to be appropriate to give, rather than what God demanded. Cain's reasoning was 'twisted'. ***This twisted reasoning went something like this:***

- I, Cain, am a farmer – I work the land.
- God wants a blood sacrifice.
- My plants do not possess blood, only animals and human beings possess blood.
- I will not sacrifice an animal because I have perfectly good plants here.
- I will give God some of my plants.
- I have worked hard to raise these beautiful plants.
- These plants are good enough for God.

Then, when God rejects the plants, Cain reasons as follows:

-How dare God accept Abel's offering of an animal and reject my plant offering?

- I have a right to be upset with God because He has clearly preferred my brother, my younger brother and his offering, over what I offered Him.

-I am angry.

-In bitterness, Cain surmises, "God prefers Abel over me."

-I'll show God. I will kill him whom God prefers.

-I have no responsibility for my brother.

-I will pay back God by killing Abel.

- I will shed his blood, the blood of my brother who has found favor with God.

The derivative thought that yielded 'twisted reasoning' began with a focus on self, not on God. Statement 1: I, Cain, am a farmer – I work the land. The truth statement that should have come first is this.

The truth is God created the heavens and the earth.

Then, God created man in His own image.

I, Cain, am one of God's creations.

He has provided me the life that I have including the ability to farm.

He, my Creator, requires a blood sacrifice.

I will comply with His request because He is God and I am not.

I did not make myself.

I could not farm if God did not make the earth.

I know what God requires.

Out of fundamental appreciation for God, I will comply.

The consequences of failing to acknowledge God lead to murder.

The consequences of acknowledging God are appreciation of life.

This fact has not changed over the millennia. Starting with truth is the most effective and efficient way to solve any problem. Partial truth dilutes the favorableness of outcome. Lies kill.

In this era of eclecticism where even much of the institution of the Church wavers on its allegiance to the inerrancy of Holy Scripture, discomfort is highest with exposure to the Holy Bible. There is genuine "dis-ease" in the secular mindset with thinking about God first. As a consequence, again, the Holy Bible is the dividing line for our nation, and the dividing line for the institutional mechanisms of the church. This controversy within the nation has implications for how the United States will fair in the international arena.

We will return to this matter in a later chapter. For now, suffice it to say that decisions rooted in biblical principles require divergence from secular frames of reference that will have internal and international implications.

Eclecticism violates the boundaries that distinguish true Christianity from other religions and the cults.

It is a fact. We are prone to wander as we deviate from God's standard of truth, the Holy Bible. Such wandering from God's Word in an abominable abandonment is often bred of political expediency.

In the Old Testament, the presence of wandering is depicted as a judgment from God. Wandering still is. It is a permitted judgment against our increased tolerance for that which is intolerable from God's perspective. The consequence of such wandering manifests itself in the form of instability, incoherence, inattentiveness – symptoms writ large as we diverge from the biblically prescribed task of securing justice, loving mercy, and walking in humility with God. It is as if we become de-railed from our spiritual train of thought because we shift our gaze. Our focus that was once on Christ blurs as we immerse ourselves in secular modes of thought to hold what is perceived to be successful conversation on our job.

Fall of Man, which points to the tragic estrangement of man and his world from their true being, an estrangement that is transferred to the *horizontal plane*.

According to Paul Tillich,

> It becomes an absurdity on the horizontal plane; it becomes a story of a human couple a few thousand years ago in what is now present-day Iraq. One of the most profound psychological descriptions of the general human predicament becomes an absurdity on the horizontal plane. If the symbols of the Savior and the salvation through Him which point to the healing power in history and

personal life are transferred to the horizontal plane, they become stories of a half-divine being coming from a heavenly place and returning to it.

If the idea of God (and the symbols applied to Him) which expresses man's ultimate concern is transferred to the horizontal plane, God becomes a being among others whose existence or nonexistence is a matter of inquiry. Nothing perhaps, is more symptomatic of the loss of the dimension or depth than the permanent discussion about the existence or nonexistence of God – the discussion itself is wrong and possible only after the loss of the dimension of depth.

When in this way man has deprived himself of the dimension of depth and the symbols expressing it, he then becomes a part of the horizontal plane. He loses his self and becomes a thing among things. He becomes an element in the process of manipulated production and manipulated consumption. This is now a pattern of public knowledge. We have become award of the degree to which everyone in our social structure is managed, even if one knows it if one belongs himself to the managing group. The influence of the gang mentality on adolescents or the corporation's demands on the executive, of the conditioning of everyone by public communication, by propaganda and advertising under the guidance of motivation research, et cetera, have all been described in many books and articles.[69]

Going a step further than Tillich, there is not only a loss of depth, superficiality associated with our God-given lives, but there is also a rejection of the idea that there is absolute truth. This leads the Church to speak of the gospel as "a good way to get to God" rather than as the only way to God.

Understanding demands a comprehensive view of the intricate relationship between current behavioral dynamics and the sequence of prior events to which individuals are reacting. That dynamic, however, is not resting upon mere human explanation. Understanding of God's description of the human malady is the fundamental understanding that is required. That perceptiveness then coupled with revelatory "knowledge," so that one may recognize and then use the tools God has made available to strategically address the past and present simultaneously, is what makes right order. What it means to maintain right order must be examined. Maintenance implies action that renders functionality. In this case, we are talking about the actions that take into consideration current conditions along with the luggage of the past. This information is to be leveraged so that the status of the components net results. The "order" has to do with each in the place that is maximally beneficial to that which defined membership originally.

One need not be a perfect human being but you must be a redeemed human being who yields to Christ if you wish to conscientiously partner with Him in His work here on earth. Right relations with God yield moral clarity and a better way of life.

FIGURE 4.1

The Deliverance Cycle
For The Nation

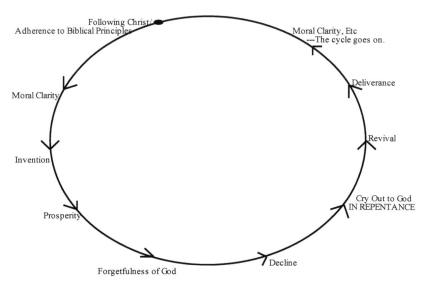

So, what is the link between the secular environment and policy agendas in prodigal societies? The answer is assumptions.

Consequences of Reliance upon Secularized Assumptions

There are many methods available in public policy literature all of which presumed useful in the making of decisions of state. Decisions synonymous with judgments, conclusions, verdicts, and resolutions to act are the hallmark of what government officials and their accompanying institutions are to do. Methods such as brainstorming, argumentative mapping, synectics, hierarchy analysis, multiple perspective analysis, classification analysis, assumption analysis, and the analysis of boundaries – all have this in common. They each presume rationality. They each presume sanity, a well reasoned, clearheaded sobriety of thought. *Reason. Logic.* The assumption is that which is commonsensical will rule the day. The academic expectation is that the grounding of argument will be sound. Theory will not rest upon flawed mental processes that are in defiance of the commonsensical. Assumed also is that ultimately, truth, even if it is only partial, will prevail. It is presumed, in essence that only the plausible will exude in the midst of the scientific and often sterile environment of "experts" spouting convergent, divergent, serial or cyclic arguments. What is not recognized, however, is that when God is not acknowledged, that which is communicated is fundamentally flawed.

According to Rabbi Twerski,

> When rational people behave improperly, it is invariably because of a lack of perception of what life is about. The Sages say, "A person does not sin unless he is overtaken by a spirit of folly. All sin is, as it were, temporary insanity, for which we are nevertheless held accountable.[70]

That is a frightening thought. What if, fundamentally this assumption of rationality is not being met? What then? Such a question considered heretical in this age of secular religion must be asked. Rationality is not assured in society at large. Furthermore, since our leadership reflects the populous, there is no assurance that reason will prevail within the corridors of power. God warns in the book of Ezekiel:

> *Son of man, you dwell in the midst of the house of the rebellious, who have eyes to see and see not, who have ears to hear and hear not, for they are a rebellious house ….*
> *Son of man, these men have set up their idols in their hearts and put the stumbling block of their iniquity and guilt before their faces; should I permit Myself to be inquired of at all by them? Therefore speak to them and say to them, Thus says the Lord God: Every man of the house of Israel who takes his idols [of self-will and un-submissiveness] into his heart and puts the stumbling block of his iniquity [idols of silver and gold] before his face, and yet comes to the prophet [to inquire of him], I the Lord will answer him, answer him according to the multitude of his idols, that I may lay hold of the house of Israel in the thoughts of their own mind and heart, because they are all estranged from Me through their idols.[71]*

Rebelliousness against God blinds and deafens. The rebellious have eyes and ears that fail them because the rebellion takes on the characteristics of idolatry, that which becomes their ultimate concern. The rebellious become as deaf and blind as the objects of their worship, which are the work of their own hands. God promises to answer in keeping with the level of idolatry practiced. The only solution to this senselessness is repentance. The right turning away from idols and back to God yields rationality.

Secularized Assumptions Yield Secular Responses

Multiculturalism - - We have a problem, Western world. We have among us individuals that are executioners who aspire to die. We have them living amongst us, in our own culture, a culture that is ever increasingly being allured itself by death and the killing of life, any life, especially the pre-born children. There is with this progression toward the destruction of that which God has imprinted His image on, a hostile force of walking dead people who are willing bomb operatives. This hostility is shared by many and poses increasing risk.

Eclecticism: A Deviation from the Biblical Foundation

It is in this era of eclecticism we must develop biblically sound policy narrative. Given this backdrop, public policy decision-making takes place. For example, the immigration debate gravitates around two opposing views. One view stresses economic market function where goods and services provided by people are exchanged between nations with less importance placed upon the national border, citizenship, or sovereignty. Instead, the focus is upon exchange rendered as functionally profitable among trading partners.

The other view is that of demography where the immigration problem is seen in terms of numbers of people with particular emphasis upon nationality and/or ethnic origin with reference to the economic ramification seen merely as rendering competition between groups for scarce resources and jobs. The market exchange function and demographic imagery considerations meet only in those incidences where reference is made to cases of sought after education/technical exchange of expertise or the need for political asylum. Meanwhile, at the domestic level within the U.S. population, conversation is most frequently one that uses language akin to physical invasion. That invasion is expressed either in terms of competing workforce for limited employment opportunities; or the problem is seen as one of an enormous number of uninvited guests. In the later case, the situation became described as physical invasion of our nation, made ever so difficult because of national security concerns. The most potent post-9/11 language used terms such as rape as these uninvited guests were perceived as making use of national privileges that they were not rightly espoused to receive.

The truth is that when a leader acknowledges God, he puts into action in line with God's plan all the force of heaven and earth for implementation. The "Royal We," would be in force. Meaning, God the Father, God the Son, God the Holy Spirit and the ruler of your nation would be in agreement about what was about to transpire. Failure to acknowledge God means that the results will be piecemeal at best because the cohering aspect of the universe would not be a part of the action. When a leader acknowledges God, such a leader becomes engaged as an authoritative covering over the population and can most effectively stand in the gap for all of those under his authority. The leader's decisions will be blessed and hence bless those who are his followers. To the extent that leaders do not acknowledge God, the populace suffers. The populace is encouraged by God to pray for those in authority so that the populace may lead a peaceable life. The best example of this principle is reflected in the account of the centurion found in the book of Matthew in the New Testament. The account given in Matthew 8:5-13 is as follows:

> *When Jesus had entered Capernaum, a centurion came to him, asking for help. "Lord," he said, "My servant lies at home paralyzed and in terrible suffering." Jesus said to him, "I will go and heal him." The centurion replied, "Lord, I do not deserve to have you come under my roof. But just say the word, and my servant will be healed. For I myself am a man under authority, with soldiers under me. I tell this one, 'Go,' and he goes; and that one, 'Come,' and he comes. I say to my servant, 'Do this,' and he does it." When Jesus heard this, he was astonished and said to those following him, "I tell you the truth, I have not found anyone in Israel with such great faith. I say to you that many will come from the east and the west, and will take their places at the feast with Abraham, Isaac and Jacob in the kingdom of heaven. But the subjects of the kingdom will be thrown outside, into the darkness, where there will be weeping and gnashing of teeth." Then Jesus said to the centurion, "Go! It will be done just as you believed it would." And his servant was healed at that very hour."[72]*

There are those that might argue that this idea of nobility of leadership is obsolescent. That, because we live in a democracy, the notion does not apply. Not so! Because in protestant reformed democracies there was an understanding of the authority of God, those who were saved reflected that authority. In being saved, those free and independent citizens by virtue of their transformation into new creations were filled with the presence of the Holy Spirit who took up residence in them, and became visible evidence of their adoption into the family of God, a child of God – the ultimate sovereign of the universe – whose Son, Christ Jesus, is the King of Kings. Each citizen was a king. And, Christ Jesus is the King of kings. With the presence of the Holy Spirit resident in each person, it was further understood that right decisions could be made because of the fruit of the Holy Spirit, especially that of self control. Additionally, the gifts of the Spirit would give that which was needed to work in harmony with God on this earth as his citizens took dominion to His honor and glory – not by power, nor by might, but by His Spirit.

The gifts of the Spirit along with the disposition of Christ which is characterized by the fruits of the Spirit were all that was needed to remain attuned to the wishes of God the Father as the citizens meditated upon Holy Scripture and put into practice the truths they learned once they accepted Jesus Christ as their Savior and Lord. That vibrant, true relationship with Christ Jesus renders moral clarity and the spiritual fortitude when institutions and society itself go askew. One is able to move independent of forces that counter the written Word of God, the Holy Bible.

Much of the controversy seen in the earlier part of the twenty-first century over the display of the Ten Commandments had to do with the uncomfortable conviction associated with those commandments if you were an unsaved person. It is impossible to keep those commandments without a vibrant relationship with Christ Jesus. When people don't have Jesus, the commandments are overwhelmingly burdensome to their way of thinking. And, in a society built upon biblical principles, those who have turned their back on biblical teachings do not want to be reminded of their waywardness. The Commandments are offensive to their fallen sensibilities.

Assessment Challenges

What differentiates the United States from other nations is the fact that Biblical foundations were the basis of this country. As a consequence, the United States has been blessed by God as a nation. We are living in the legacy of that foundation in a nation that is unrivaled in quality of life by any other nation on the face of this earth. As you consider the implications of the secular perspective on any policy issue, it is important to keep in mind the fact that a number of assessment challenges exist ahead.

TABLE 4.1
ASSESSMENT CHALLENGES[73]

The preoccupation with public opinion polls and human initiatives devoid of Godly wisdom has left the decision-making apparatus of that which was founded upon biblical principles impotent. The deficiency is most evident in the failure to adequately address the following challenges confronting us in the public arena:

1. Development of unambiguous measures of progress
2. Goal misspecification/wording and ambiguity
3. Contradictory goals
4. Impact (positive and negative) of goal change –transformation linked to the political economy of organizations
5. Serving multiple constituencies
6. Negative limitations of established goals
7. Absence of universally accepted means of judging the value of what is produced
8. Measurement of nonevents and counterfactual occurrences
9. Activity measures being substituted for output measures when attempting to evaluate performance
10. Government performance measures generally inhibited by time span for achievement of benefits, determining the durability of action results, and political difficulties.[74]

Human Reasoning

God admonishes us in Proverbs 3:1-6 by stating the following:

"My son, do not forget my teaching, but keep my commands in your heart, for they will

*prolong your life many years and bring you prosperity. Let love and faithfulness never
leave you; bind them around your neck, write them on the tablet of your heart. Then
you will win favor and a good name in the sight of God and man. Trust in the LORD
with all your heart and lean not on your own understanding; in all your ways
acknowledge Him, and He will make your paths straight."*

The problem is that many fail to recognize the connection between right acknowledgement
of God and the quality of life the population experiences under the authority of its leadership.
What follows are the public policy mechanisms that break down then right relationship with
God is absent. Failure to acknowledge God's rule has adverse consequences.

"Fear of the LORD is the Beginning of Wisdom."

Biblically sound public policy recommendations maximize the likelihood of receptivity
of proposals even among those who do not share a biblical worldview. This is accomplished by
explaining *(i)* the futility of effort; *(ii)* the points of access within the policymaking process that
lend themselves to the introduction of ideas consistent with biblical principles; *(iii)* the nature of
biblically sound policy narrative; and *(iv)* means for generating biblically driven evaluation of
public policy, its implementation and impact.

According to Wycliffe, *the Holy Bible is government of the people, by the people and for the people.*
That being said, for the rest of the nations of the world, the U.S. model is relevant only in this regard: The
Constitutional designers acknowledged God. And, "He [GOD] promises that if we acknowledge Him,
He will make our paths straight." This is true for nations as well as individuals. [76]

God-fearing people designed the government. And, God says that the fear of the
Lord is the beginning of Wisdom. That is why the details of the U.S. constitution and its provisions
are framed with appropriate durability.

It is relationship with God that will make the difference. As far as nation building goes,
it will not do to simply transport the U.S. Constitution into another setting. What is required is
relationship with God that will yield Divine revelation from Him concerning the establishment
of a relevant constitution for the nation. As with the founders of the United States, it was not
human ingenuity but divine inspiration that led to nature of our document for this country.

God is no respecter of persons and will grant abundant wisdom to any who ask.

With the development of working documents, first to acknowledge the tyranny associated with business as usual; and then, second to succinctly address those areas that are crippling that nation, you will then be able to present an alternative agenda to the nation---an agenda endorsed by God. Since He is the one that establishes authority throughout the world, it is important that framers of an emerging government not kick against the goad. Failure at national repentance yields the outcome of increased corruption and accompanying economic, social, and political instability in any nation. And, remember, the leader is a mirror of the nation at large.

ACTION POINT

Finding the Scriptural Address of the Problem[77]

Of course, study the Word of God to understand who we are and who God has equipped us to be. But, also, test every idea on the basis of the Bible.

Jesus Christ said of Himself, *"I only do the things I see My Father doing."* John 5:19, *Holy Bible*. I believe that is what we need to do, too!

It behooves us to prayerfully consult the Holy Bible to find the scriptural address of the topic of interest. In my case, I am interested in exploring elements associated with correcting organizational activity. Here is how I approached the question during my study of the Holy Bible. I found the scriptural address to be Chapter 1 of Genesis. That passage discusses God creating order out of chaos. Consider the following:

When we read Chapters 1 of Genesis we find a pattern of making order out of chaos. For your convenience, Chapter 1 is presented here.
"In the beginning God created the heavens and the earth.
#1-[*Recognition of God as Creator, the Source of origin*]

Now the earth was formless and empty, darkness was over the surface of the deep, and the Spirit of God was hovering over the waters.
#2-[*Recognition of the actual state of affairs, all of its important attributes, along with the tools God has made available to address the issues at hand.*]

And God said, 'Let there be light,' and there was light.
#3-[*Execute actions that support visibility, the ability to see things as they really are*]

REMEMBER: "The word of God is a lamp unto our feet and a light unto our path."
All ideas/proposals must rightly align with what is written in the Holy Bible, Saints.

God saw that the light was good, and he separated the light from the darkness.
#4-[*Determine whether or not that which is used to make visible the status is good,
valid, reliable, reflective of the TRUTH. And, if it is good, separate that which enables
visibility from that which obscures or otherwise inhibits the needed visibility.*]

God called the light 'day,' and the darkness he called 'night.'
#5-[*Label the difference*]

And, there was evening, and there was morning—the first day.
#6-[*Be cognizant of time in relation to the tool of visibility*]

And God said, 'Let there be a vault between the waters to separate water from water.' #7-
[*Sort, differentiating with relevant precision--not just lumping like things together, but
identifying relevant differences and sorting accordingly.*]

So, God made the vault and separated the water under the vault from the water above it.
#8-[*Create a means of separating the differentiated elements.*]

And it was so.
#9-[*Come to completion on differentiation*]

God called the vault 'sky.' And there was evening, and there was morning—the second day.
[*Label while remaining cognizant of your use of time.*]

And God said, 'Let the water under the sky be gathered to one place, and let dry ground appear.'
#10-[*Put like items in a shared location different from other things.*]

And it was so.
#11-[*Come to completion on placement.*]

God called the dry ground 'land,' and the gathered waters he called 'seas.'
#12-[*Label*]

And God saw that it was good.
#13-[*Assess what you have done so far.*]

Then God said, 'Let the land produce vegetation: seed-bearing plants and trees on the land that
bear fruit with seed in it, according to their various kinds.'
#14-[*Take what you have and set up conditions for fruitful production, meaning identify that
which has within itself all that is needed to reproduce, and organize that production according to its
kind.*]

And it was so.

#15-[*Assess how you have set up the conditions in which production is to take place*]

The land produced vegetation: plants bearing seed according to their kinds and trees bearing fruit with seed in it according to their kinds.
#16-[*Determine whether there is a right match between what is to be produced where and the kind of yield expected.*]

And God saw that it was good.
#17-[*Look at this initiative in context to determine whether or not it is good.*]
And there was evening, and there was morning—the third day.
#18-[*Be cognizant of time. Mark it.*]

And God said, 'Let there be lights in the vault of the sky to separate the day from the night, and let them serve as signs to mark sacred times, and days and years, and let them be lights in the vault of the sky to give light on the earth.'
#20-[*Apply the yardstick of visibility as the gauge for assessing categories of actions, routines, operation of productivity over time.*]

And it was so.
#21-[*Come to completion in the development of that gauge.*]

God made two great lights—the greater light to govern the day and the lesser light to govern the night.
#22-[*Develop signals differencing stages of the work: stages of high visibility and low visibility.*]

He also made the stars.
#23-[*Develop elementary indicators to monitor during periods of low visibility.*]

God set them in the vault of the sky to give light on the earth, to govern the day and the night, and to separate light from darkness.
#24-[*Use indicators*]

And God saw that it was good. And there was evening, and there was morning—the fourth day.
#25-[*Assess those indicators and remain cognizant of time. Mark it.*]

And God said, 'Let the water teem with living creatures, and let birds fly above the earth across the vault of the sky.'
#26-[*Populate with that which is best suited for the environment/structure/operation you have created.*]

So God created the great creatures of the sea and every living thing with which the water teems and that moves about in it, according to their kinds, and every winged bird according to its kind.
#27-[*Populate according to kind.*]

And God saw that it was good.
#28-[*Assess population fit.*]

God blessed them and said, 'Be fruitful and increase in number and fill the water in the seas,

and let the birds increase on the earth.'
#29-[*Establish conditions favorable for reproducibility according to kind in the first structures you created*].

And there was evening, and there was morning—the fifth day.
#30-[*Remain cognizant of time. Mark it.*]

And God said, 'Let the land produce living creatures according to their kinds: the livestock, the creatures that move along the ground, and the wild animals, each according to its kind.'
#31-[*Establish conditions conducive to reproduction according to kind in the secondary structures produced.*]

And it was so.
#32-[*Come to completion on initiating populations.*]

God made the wild animals according to their kinds, the livestock according to their kinds, and all the creatures that move along the ground according to their kinds.
#33-[*Make sure initiated populations are according to kind.*]

And God saw that it was good.
#34-[*Assess the populating process.*]

Then God said, 'Let us make mankind in our image, in our likeness, so that they may rule over the fish in the sea and the birds in the sky, over the livestock and all the wild animals, and over all the creatures that move along the ground.'
#35-[*Mentor or apprentice folks you have prayerfully chosen, of like mind to yourself, and teach them all you know.*]

So God created mankind in his own image, in the image of God he created them; male and female he created them.
#36-[*Recognize the different roles and capabilities of those you have mentored.*]

God blessed them and said to them, "Be fruitful and increase in number; fill the earth and subdue it.
#37-[*Put apprentices in positions to be productive applying what they have learned, and let them reproduce the process replicating themselves.*]

Rule over the fish in the sea and the birds in the sky and over every living creature that moves on the ground.'
#38-[*Give your apprentices charge over specific populations.*]

Then God said, 'I give you every seed-bearing plant on the face of the whole earth and every tree that has fruit with seed in it.
#39- [*Instruct apprentices on how to become self-sustaining given all that was created.]*

They will be yours for food.

#40-[*Recognize and communicate what is consumable for sustainment.*]

And to all the beasts of the earth and all the birds in the sky and all the creatures that move along the ground—everything that has the breath of life in it—I give every green plant for food.'
#41-[*Identify all assets available to sustain those you have given charge.*]

And it was so.
#42-[*Come to completion on this.*]

God saw all that he had made, and it was very good. And there was evening, and there was morning — the sixth day."
#43-[*Assess the entire operation.*]

The above constitute the steps I have prayerfully derived from reading Genesis 1 of the Holy Bible.

In that Bible passage we see that God took that which was out of order and created that which would be fruitful by design. Let us do likewise in the spheres of influence God has assigned us. Let us be productive in our work by first rightly ordering our soul by rightly acknowledging God in every aspect of our life. And, as we do so, God can direct our steps as we govern to His glory.

Please check all that has been written here on the basis of Holy Scripture.

CHAPTER FIVE

Acknowledging God in Problem Redefinition and Response

"He who does not gather-- scatters."-Matthew 12:30, Holy Bible[78]

"Where is the wise man (the philosopher)? Where is the scribe (the scholar)? Where is the investigator (the logician, the debater) of this present age? Has not God shown up the nonsense and folly of this world's wisdom?"[79] *1Corinthians 1:20, Holy Bible*

Pattern of Futility Revisited.

Recall the following propositions regarding governance:

> *Proposition 1:* The solution to the declared problem will be more reflective of the problem's original, biblically sound, definition at the inception of a public policy than over time.

> *Proposition 2:* As time progresses, the numbers of actors involved in the process of problem resolution increase.

> *Proposition 3*: As time progresses, the diversity of actors involved in the process of problem resolution increase.

> *Proposition 4:* Actor diversity yields problem redefinition.

Proposition 5: With diversity, problem definition administratively changes.

Proposition 6: The original problem appears more complex with privatization.

Proposition 7: The original problem appears more complex due to expert status.

Proposition 8: Incorrect problem definition yields the public policy spiral.

What follows is an elaboration on the above propositions.

Proposition 1: The solution to the declared problem will be more reflective of the problem's original (biblically sound) definition at the inception of a public policy than over time.

Redesigning Policy Agendas in Prodigal Societies

Right relationship with God will make the difference. Once the critical spiritual issues have been addressed, then change can occur. As mentioned in earlier chapters, the typical steps are as follows:

- Discussions about rights and responsibilities of the citizenry
- Discussions about the structure of government that will maximize the preservation of the aforementioned rights
- The above discussion should be moderated with the understanding that the reason for government is not personal gain for leadership, but service that secures the rights that have been clearly outlined
- Governmental mechanisms for the purpose of securing the rights of the populace can mean the development of institutional mechanisms designed to do the following:
- Protect what is valuable to the society from threat of depletion, erosion, or obsolescence

- -Prop up that which is weak yet valued by the society
- -Forestall that which would weaken the society
- -Reacquire that which has been lost, captured, or otherwise rendered inaccessible to the society
- -Prevent adverse factors from reaching a level in which they might jeopardize the existence of rights and conditions required for those rights to prevail
- -Interrelate the derivative goals to maximize coverage, quality, and stability of those rights
- -Regulate actions, actors, and outcomes that have competing interpretations of exercise of these rights

All of the above refers to establishing or re-establishing the internal workings of the society. There is however, also the external component that is to maximize the national integrity/security of a nation.

There is a need to explore security challenges to identify current status and corresponding thresholds of acceptability for each major international security concern. The activity of specifying a recognizable threshold, a standard below which security must not fall, is part of what can be referred to as the process of problem decomposition.

Proposition 2: As time progresses, the numbers of actors involved in the process of problem resolution increase.

Proposition 3: As time progresses, the diversity of actors involved in the process of problem resolution increase.

Proposition 4: Actor diversity yields problem redefinition.

---A Good or Bad Public Policy Decision Begets Another Good or Bad Public Policy Decision---

Problem Decomposition

Problem decomposition is a procedure associated with decision analysis that allows varying stakeholders to create a scale or tradeoffs that serve to document degrees of progress or failure in the achievement of specified goals. Let's take a look at an example of what can go wrong.

Public policy decisions made today are a by-product of past decisions and past decision rules. Such progression is well documented with many scholarly careers built upon charting the routine update. The current port scenario is no different. With past decisions and prevailing decision rules come the less frequently discussed assumptions establishing the framework within which decisions are made.

Of course, we have the problem of cognitive misperception that can permeate not only leadership but also the general public. Complicating the works is the propensity to misjudge reality in group decision-making settings which is even further amplifies with perceived risk and the fear of crisis.

TABLE 5.1

ELEMENTS OF FOREIGN AND DOMESTIC POLICY INTERACTION

- ---Declaration of societal goals

- ---Social audit or assessment of societal status (internally and externally)

- ---Identification of discrepancy between declared goals and status

- ---Determination about whether any detected discrepancy between current status and declared goals is problematic through the development of a litmus test that from a decision-making perspective may involve quantifiable indicators

- ---Indicators Internal and External to the nation may use thresholds, notions of tolerance and a system for monitoring severity of conditions

- ---Identification of problem cause

- ---Agreement upon indicators that reveal the presence of both problem and cause

- ---Design of policy strategies based on theory pertaining to the cause of the problem

- ---Development and review of indicators of policy execution

- ---Specificity of monitoring points for operation phases and stages

- ---Development and execution of corrective action where deficient operation exists

- ---Identification of indicators of summative impact of overall operation on the presence of the problem

- ---Identification of indicators of impact of overall operation on the presence of the problem within the organization context of all other entities and initiatives that are designed to address aspects of the same problem

- ---Measurement of discrepancy, accountability, and change at each major junction of policy decision making.

Greater consideration should be given to how we are to measure of progress in this age. Thresholds of acceptability in action along with perceived risk in a world of public policy grounded futuristic scenarios needs to be discussed. This is especially true because government decision-making structure dictates limiting the number of factors considered when our leaders are trying to decide what to do next. [80]

Consider:

Proposition 5: With diversity and problem redefinition come administrative change

Proposition 6: The original problem appears more complex with privatization.

Proposition 7: The original problem appears even more complex due to expert status.

Proposition 8: Incorrect problem definition yields the public policy spiral.

---Demographic Imagery Tends to Dominate Public Policy Issues--

Because of humanistic reasoning, demographic imagery tends to dominate how public policy issues are viewed. A difficulty with taking purely a humanistic approach to decision-making in the policy context is that public policy spirals result.

Explanation plus Implementation

The spiral is a direct result of problem misspecification. The rate of growth associated with the spiral is further enhanced by the possible misspecification of implementation strategy. As I posited earlier, since action should be explanation driven [otherwise action would be simply mania], only one of two possible scenarios in varying configurations is likely to occur as a consequence of senseless, non-recognition of God for any policy initiative: either (1) flawed explanation yielding flawed action---flawed in the since of having either partial elements of truth , incomplete, held with apparent correctness of form, yet possessing significant gaps in understanding thus compromising our ability to arrive at appropriate solutions to problems; or, (2)flawed because we have correct explanation offered in such a vacuum as its implementation cannot be achieved because the parts that would do the implementation suffer from a lack of cohering truth. The outcomes I have described are opposite ends of a continuum. When graphically depicted [Figure 5.1], the scenario option consist of four quadrants: I -Correct Explanation/Coherent Implementation; II-Correct Explanation/Incoherent Implementation; III-Flawed Explanation/Coherent Implementation; and, IV--Flawed Explanation/Incoherent Implementation.

FIGURE 5.1

EXPLANATION PLUS IMPLEMENTATION GRID IN RELATION TO PROPOSITIONS/EXPECTED OUTCOMES

PROBLEM EXPLANATION

IMPLEMENTATION	CORRECT	FLAWED
COHERENT	I	III
INCOHERENT	II	IV

There is a relationship between Quadrant and status in the policy spiral.

Quad I – Correct Explanation/Coherent Implementation-E-1

Quad II–Correct Explanation/Incoherent Implementation-E-2-E-6

Quad III-Flawed Explanation/Coherent Implementation-E-7-E-9

Quad IV-Flawed Explanation/Incoherent ImplementationE10-E12

Greater consideration should be given to how we are to measure of progress in this age. Thresholds of acceptability in action along with perceived risk in a world of public policy grounded futuristic scenarios needs to be discussed. This is especially true because government decision-making structure dictates limiting the number of factors considered when our leaders are trying to decide what to do next. [81]

Consider:

Proposition 5: With diversity and problem redefinition comes administrative change.

Proposition 6: The original problem appears more complex with privatization.

Proposition 7: The original problem appears even more complex due to expert status.

Proposition 8: Incorrect problem definition yields the public policy spiral.

The spiral results in the futility of effort God refers to that is a direct consequence failing to acknowledge Him.   Again, the adverse by-products of spiral activity includes the challenge of (1) Competing Problem Definition; (2) Non-Problem Status; and, (3) Problem Distancing. We will now turn to an elaboration on each of these three themes in response to policy actors and actions.

TABLE 5.2

Dynamic of Public Policy Genealogy: Problem Incongruence Leading to the Policy Spiral

I. Competing Problem Definitions

- The creation of any policy has an interactive effect on the existence of other policies.

- These policies may work at cross-purposes in different and shared domains.

- Focus upon one problem and its accompanying policy may serve as a distraction from other problems or policies.

- The professed problem itself may be merely symptomatic of another or a cluster of other problems not acknowledged or less visible.

- The alternative definitions may require alternative strategies that have disparate effects upon different subpopulations.

- Rarely are there single determinants of a problem yet policy tends to take single focus with multiple channels for the single focus.

- Competing definitions pose dramatic challenge of single focus initiatives.

- Compartmentalization of competing definitions allows for policy implementation diversity and diffusion of responsibility.

- To the extent that the problems require service sequences that go beyond this compartmentalization, there is service failure.

- Failure will not be acknowledged because success is measured in terms of number served domestically and number of dollar value of amount captured from international sources.

II. Non-Problem Status – Disparately Problematic

- A problem exists if there is a perceived risk associated with the existence of a phenomenon.

- A problem exists where there are identifiable stakeholders acknowledged as requiring its solution.

- A problem exists if there is a consensus about the nature of the problem.

- A problem is a non-problem if the problem is acknowledged and no action or symbolic/superficial action is taken.

- A problem is a non-problem if resources are continuously expended with the same result of ineffectiveness being witnessed.

- A problem is a non-problem if the stakeholders are not acknowledged as being significant.

- A problem is a non-problem if it is permitted to exist or increase in intensity with no measurable change in level of activity effectively directed at its eradication.

- A problem is a non-problem if it is defined as something other than what it truly is.

- A problem is a non-problem if its solution in no way resembles and/or accommodates its professed definition

III. Problem Distancing – The Policy Implementation Spiral

- There exists a reciprocal relation between policy and policy implementation.

- The reciprocal relation serves to expand and thicken the administrative aspects of problems over time.

- The expansion and increased density of the administrative aspect of policy has a rate of change that is directly correlated with the amount of time that has transpired since the problem was originally acknowledged.

- The time factor allows for the distancing of strategy for problem eradication to distance itself from the original conceptualization of the problem.

- The implication is that the longer the problem is acknowledged, the less likely there is a relation between policy and implementation that addresses the nature of the original problem.

- With the inclusion of each administrative subpart, the problem becomes redefined administratively.

- The theory that originally held in the justification of policy fails to be relevant as time passes.

- Additionally, with the momentum of relation and activity of policy to implementation strategy, it is possible to detect the impact of pull or centrifugal force associated with the administrative aspect of policy implementation.

- This force tends to pull in originally unrelated administrative actors into the fury of new and diverse organizations and roles making denser the original administrative apparatus.

For application, consider the US-Iraq case. The initial stages appear below. Missing the mark in terms of problem definition poses lasting challenges.

TABLE 5.3

US-Iraq Public Policy Spiral—Labeled Aspects

Events   *Dates*

PROBLEM DEFINED

-Terrorist Attack the United States   September 11, 2001

-Iraq war planned while hunting Osama bin Laden   December 28, 2001

Principle Actors: President Bush and Army General Tommy Franks

AGENDA ANNOUNCED

-Announcement by President Bush to dismantle Saddam Hussein's regime   July 8, 2002

IMPLEMENTATION

-Saddam Hussein captured   December 13, 2003

-Abu Ghraib prison photographs emerge pointing to prisoner abuse   April 2004

-Iraqi interim government receives authority from the U.S.   June 28, 2004

STATUS REPORT

-Report from U.S. Arms Inspector finds no evidence of weapons   October 6, 2004

of mass destruction

-Approval of the Iraqi constitution   October 15, 2005

MORE ACTORS INTRODUCED

-Iraqi Parliament Elections   December 15, 2005

-Dome of a Shi-it shrine in Samarra was destroyed   February 23, 2006

-Additional US troops are sent to Baghdad   August   2006

EXPERTS REPORT

-Reports from US military recommend refocus in Baghdad   October 2006

PROBLEM DEFINITION CHANGE

-Republicans lose control of the Senate and the House of   November 7, 2006
Representatives

-President Bush announces Rumsfeld resignation   November 8, 2006

-Robert Gates nominated by President Bush to be Rumsfeld's   November 8, 2006
successor

FISCAL EXPANSION

-President Bush announces the sending of 21, 500 additional   January 10, 2007
troops to Iraq

ACTIONS OF ADDITIONAL ACTORS

- A nonbinding resolution opposing the additional troops to be   January 31, 2007
sent to was proposed by Senators Carl Levin, Democrat
from Michigan and Senators John Warner, Republican
from Virginia

-Full Senate debate on nonbinding resolution blocked by   February 5, 2007
Republicans

ACTION POINT

Consider the following template for the development of a case study of a pivotal event.

CASE STUDY TEMPLATE[82]

1. What are the background issues that led to the Critical Event?

History -

Recent Events-

Response Timeline-

Intervention-

Multi-Level Check Point-

2. Was there anything about the specific nation that would make it more susceptible to crisis than other nations?

History-

Pre-Existing Challenges-

Prior Attempts at Resolution-

Assessment-

Added Challenges Posed by the Critical Event-

Obstacles to Response-

Implications-

Outcome Compared to Comparable Scenarios in Other Locations-

3. What role did the international community play in the event sequence? Was it appropriate? Did it help or hinder outcome?

Timeline of Events-

Typical Plan/Decision Points for Intervention-

Typical Decision Rules and Why-

What Parameters Determined Actions in the Specific Nation-

Sequence of Actors/Organizations Introduced into Crisis Response-

Answer to the above questions

4. What are the lasting implications of this crisis for the nation in question and for neighboring nations?

Governance/Law & Order

Quality of Life

Immigration

Youth

Long-Term Implications

5. What are the lessons to be desired from the sequence of events and attempted interventions and for whom?

Anticipated Sequence of Intervention

Actual Sequence of Intervention

Actors and Actions at Each Point in the Sequence

Consequences and Implications at Each Juncture

Formative Evaluation

Summative Evaluation

Conclusion for the Specific Nation

Lessons Learned for Collaboration

6. What were the critical turning points that could have changed the outcome?

Pre-Crisis Status

Pre-Crisis Turning Points

Crisis

Immediate Post Crisis Status

Post Crisis Turning Points

Conclusion of the Matter

Lessons Learned

7. What obstacles or points of decision were instrumental in yielding the current outcome?

-List of Decision Points

-Outcome at Each Decision Point

-Lessons to be Learned Concerning Each Obstacle

Implication for Future Action Plans

8. How could those obstacles be avoided?

-Detailed Nature of Each Obstacle

-What Brought About the Obstacle?

9. What were the dominant attributes of key decision-makers?

10. What were the key decision points?

11. What operative assumptions and facts influenced the choice of approach taken by the various stakeholders?

12. What were the points of conflict?

13. How might the nation's crisis and subsequent scenarios be avoided in the future?

14. What would have to be in place in terms of civilian capacity and military relations to have prevented this series of scenarios?

15. What indicators of susceptibility to crisis require monitoring, by whom, and in what areas?

16. What A-->B-->C yielded the specific nation's status?

17. How have these events reshaped the nation?

18. What are the attributes of the specific case that are generally agreed upon?

19. What do supporters of the ouster point to as justification?

20. What can others learn from the specific case?

21. How have each of the major stakeholders been tested in the specific case?

22. What were the stakeholder clashes?

23. What was the key point of conflict?

24. When did the crisis peak?

25. How has nation changed from that point on?

26. Please assess the following relationships:

----stakeholder to stakeholder

----stakeholder to crisis

----change in position among individual stakeholders

----change in the central stakeholder

27. How is this crisis resolved?

28. What did this crisis reveal about the stakeholders, the institutions, the specific nation, the international community at-large, and the United States in particular?

29. What has been the internal and external change for the nation and surrounding nations as a consequence?

CHAPTER 6

Acknowledging God in Response to Actors and Actions

---

*"**The** [intrinsically] good man produces what is good and honorable and moral **out of the** good treasure [stored] in his **heart**; and **the** [intrinsically] evil man produces what is wicked and depraved **out of the** evil [in his **heart**]; for his **mouth speaks from the overflow of his heart**."[83] Matthew 12:34, Holy Bible, Amplified Version*

Many fail to recognize the connection between right acknowledgment of God and the quality of life the population experiences under the authority of its leadership. This book points to the public policy mechanisms that break down when right relationship with God is absent. Failure to acknowledge God's rule has adverse consequences. Both believer and unbeliever are invited to see for themselves the results of acknowledging God in the decisions of state. Willard makes this point. "God as personality is not a physical reality that everyone must see whether they want to or not. He can, of course, make himself present to the human mind in any way he chooses. But, for good reasons rooted deeply in the nature of the person and of personal relationships-his preferred way is to speak, to communicate: thus the absolute centrality of scripture to our discipleship. And this, among other things, is the reason why an extensive use of solitude and silence is so basic for growth of the human spirit, for they form an appropriate context for listening and speaking to God."[84] Given that reality, the acknowledgment of God is not simply and ceremonial act by a real transformation on the heart and mind of the individual so that in right relationship with Christ, the mind is transformed and sanity is restored. As a consequence, a disciple is someone who is learning from Jesus how to live this life.

Redeeming the Policy Conversation

The preoccupation with public opinion polls and human initiatives devoid of Godly wisdom has left the decision-making lacking.

Designing Biblically Sound Policy Narratives:
Points of Entry Associated with Assessment Challenges

A characteristic of foreign policy, making that policy arena unique, is the fact that foreign policy has been best depicted as a pendulum that repeatedly swings to and fro from a posture of isolationism to a posture of interventionism. By isolationism, scholars are referring to periods in which the United States directs its attention and resources toward internal issues of the country and its populace. On the other hand, by interventionism, it is meant that the country is actively seeking to protect or secure that which is either threatened or politically, and if need be, militarily attainable for the interest of the country. There have been various motivations for interventionism, not the least of which has been the concern for trade expansionism.

Climb with me to the highest point from which you can view the full spectrum of events that shape the thinking of those who claim, "Religion is the cause of violence throughout the world." Those that make that claim do so by pointing to the violence that accompanies ethnic, racial, and religious division. That claim is made at a time when political polarity is a by-product of a stated national stance toward Jerusalem; any national reference to God especially in governing constitutions; and, against our national response to transnational actors who have made a one-sided declaration of "holy war" against the United States. In such a politically charged climate, President George W.

Bush made a very interesting statement that summarizes in part his foreign policy position. President Bush said, "Religious freedom means peace."

Foreign and domestic policy remain philosophically intertwined foundationally on the operative belief that all religions, philosophies, and gods are created equal. Eclecticism is the product of horizontal thinking. It focuses on social manipulation of many rather than the vertical depth required to answer the profound questions of life all originating from our separation from God, and hence the separation of humanity from its true self. The challenge to the domestic concerns stem frequently from the move to compartmentalize faith, to separate it from basic functions of governance. Individual decisions will have to be made regarding how one places oneself with regard to the controversy over the inerrancy of scripture because the God of the Bible through the convicting presence of His Holy Spirit will not allow us to remain neutral.

Decisions are the result of explanation (theory), and as such all action is the consequence of decision based upon the acceptance of explanation. Decision is theory-driven, thus making rational action decision-driven. If the explanation (theory) is wrong, the action will be faulty at best. It is possible, as a result of God's grace, to have a favorable outcome despite the initial error in thought. But, when it does happen, it is a miracle in the literal sense of the word. God said that we were to take dominion of this earth. We were to name things, assigning meaning to that which God presents to us. It is an issue of kingdom authority, defining various aspects of life. The definition that proceeds without right acknowledgement of God possesses within itself seeds of adversity. What follows are Providential points of opportunity to infuse corrective action.

As mentioned before, a key difficulty with taking purely a humanistic approach to decision-making in the policy context is that public policy spirals result. If you recall, the characteristics of public policy cycle, the spirals and assessment challenges, the combination tends to occur as follows. One should identify the stage and corresponding spiral effects and challenge to target focused prayer for God's wisdom and intervention. In Table 6.1 the Stage in the policy process is presented followed by the events (E) that take place at that stage within the policy spiral. Finally, presented is the assessment challenge that must be prayerfully addressed at that juncture within the policy cycle.[85] So, now let's consider correction.

GETTING BACK ON TRACK!

Consider Table 6.1.

TABLE 6.1
PUBLIC POLICY CYCLE, POLICY SPIRAL EVIDENCE, AND FOCUSED STRATEGY FOR ADDRESSING ASSESSMENT CHALLENGES

---Declaration of societal goals

E-1 Solution to the declared problem will be most reflective of its original (biblically sound) definition prior to the inception of planned strategy to address the problem.

FOCUSED STRATEGY----Development of unambiguous measures of progress

---Social audit or assessment of societal status (internally and externally)

E-2 As time progresses there will be an increase in actors involved in the resolution of this problem

FOCUSED STRATEGY ----Avoidance of goal misspecification/wording and ambiguity

---Identification of discrepancy between declared goals and status

E-3 As time progresses and the number and more importantly the diversity of actors increases so does the definition of the problem administratively change for both the implementers and the clients that rely in part of the clues to understanding their problem by the definition imposed upon them administratively.

FOCUSED STRATEGY----Avoidance of contradictory goals

---Determination about whether any detected discrepancy between current status and declared goals is problematic through the development of a litmus test that from a decision-making perspective may involve quantifiable indicators

E-4 Diversity brings with it problems of turf and language as well as personalities.

FOCUSED STRATEGY----Measurement of impact (positive and negative) of goal change – transformation linked to the political economy of organizations
---Indicators Internal and External to the nation may use thresholds, notions of tolerance and a system for monitoring severity of conditions

TABLE 6.1 CONTINUED

E-5 Problem is made more complex with privatization because there is no central focus or accountability with regard to the use of not for profit volunteers. Instead, volunteerism marks the degree of fluidity of the implementation mechanism used.

FOCUSED STRATEGY----Develop biblical sound commonality of thread serving multiple constituencies
---**Identification of problem cause**

E-6 With the infusion of the administrative actors into the policy conversation by virtue of expert status, the policy evolves.

FOCUSED STRATEGY----Identify the negative limitations of established goals
---**Agreement upon indicators that reveal the presence of both problem and cause**

E-7 An incorrect problem definition leaves its mark in the spiral because it represents the original starting point from which all other policy modifications must evolve. In essence the assumptions continue even when the operations change hence giving way to the opportunity for the organizations or units within an organization to work at cross-purposes.

FOCUSED STRATEGY----Establish a biblically sound and universally understood narrative as criteria as the means of judging the value of what is produced
---**Design of policy strategies based on theory pertaining to the cause of the problem**

E-8 The final outcome is that the client is left out of the mix of policy and implementation as time progresses. The vision becomes more internally focused upon survival and expansion of the administrative apparatus given the presence of an increasing number of competitive organizations. Indeed, there is nothing to be gained by being responsive give the whirlwind of activity.

FOCUSED STRATEGY----Develop biblically sound counterfactual measures of nonevents
---**Development and review of indicators of policy execution**

E-9 At a time of fiscal constraint the variable of time is accelerated with the administrative adjustments to capture and retain certain turf. Policy elements such as eligibility criteria become more visible and degree of plight becomes less obvious.

FOCUSED STRATEGY----Develop biblically sound output measures when attempting to evaluate performance
---**Specificity of monitoring points for operation phases and stages**

TABLE 6.1 CONTINUED

E-10 Policy is transformed administratively to constrict the number of persons directly affected by its administrative arm to preserve the existence of the actors that survive.

FOCUSED STRATEGY ----Introduce NATHANS to Government officials to offer bible study and guidance on biblically sound performance measures generally inhibited by time span for achievement of benefits, determining the durability of action results, and political difficulties

---**Development and execution of corrective action where deficient operation exists**

E-11 With the amount of acceleration of relation between policy and implementation comes the increased likelihood of attachment to other spirals so that a hurricane effect occurs where the underlying premises are shared by the draping of one perceived "true" policy assumption like the power of punitive measures as being also appropriate in the domestic as it was in the international arena. Hence, war success to punish a nation is al seen as appropriate as a strategy to punish other "offenders" of society's rules such as those selling and using drugs, etc.

FOCUSED STRATEGY----Practice biblically sound cognitive exercise that may be applied to difficulty questions in order to isolate the effects of multiple programs

---**Identification of indicators of summative impact of overall operation on the presence of the problem**

---**Identification of indicators of impact of overall operation on the presence of the problem within the organization context of all other entities and initiatives that are designed to address aspects of the same problem**

---**Measurement of discrepancy, accountability, and change at each major junction of policy decision making.**

E-12 The consequences for the poor are that unless the original problem definition is on the mark, there is no way to administratively solve the problem with time.   But, more importantly, even if it is on the mark, the amount of effectiveness of the policy will be dependent upon the administrative arm that will only temporarily be concerned with the issues associated with tem. The interactive effect of policy and implementation absorbs attention and distracts from the original mission.

FOCUSED STRATEGY   ----Biblically sound social strategies to overcome the limitations on evaluation due to organizational bias, i.e. omitting review of unintended consequences. *******

Macro explanations of reality that we typically call theories can be tested. Those explanations that become recognized as true are the ones upon which we should act.

It is no accident to encounter resistance to the "idea" of absolute truth, nor an accompanying disdain for the tools used to assess/test the truthfulness of claims. Problem misspecification renders a design that addresses at best mere symptoms of more fundamental problems. Serious bible study and prayer is needed to consider God-honoring options to avoid problem misspecification.

TABLE 6.2

EXAMPLE OF TOPICS FOR BIBLICALLY-INFORMED RECONSIDERATION

- Internationally accepted norms consistent with prevailing religious standards of conduct;
- Ethnic, racial, and religious polarization;
- Treatment of prisoners and religious artifacts;
- International watchdogs, humanitarian assistance, and global interest groups;
- Natural and unnatural disaster response strategies including the monitoring of flow of funds to prevent
- money from falling into the wrong hands;
- Medical concerns and the threat of biological terrorism;
- Language and diplomacy;
- Interpretation of well-being, safety, and the respect for law; and of course,
- Factors contributing to the presence of "Failed States"

Independent of the nature of questions posed, we know that *"All scripture is given by inspiration of God, and is profitable for doctrine, for reproof, for correction, for instruction in righteousness; that the man of God may be perfect, thoroughly furnished unto all good works."*[86] Amen!

ACTION POINT

You may have heard the story of the five blind men, each touching some part of the elephant. One has the trunk, one has the leg, one has the ears, one has the tail, and one has the tongue. Their collective knowledge of what constitutes the elephant renders a description that misses the biggest part of the animal. Such is the case with the accelerated erosive nature of shared perspectives that do not have access to the God's wisdom--- the comprehensively coherent discernment that only God can enable. This book discusses the processes at work that come from starting off with human opinion as a way of understanding the dynamics that are shaping our world. Failure to Acknowledge God means that we will miss the mark. We will increase the likelihood of accepting as the full truth that which is only an aspect of that truth. We will accept as the key mere the symptoms of problems. Vision obscured by our failure to acknowledge God in our decision-making presents the most telling problem in the governance of our nation. On an individual level, we can see the devastation that can result from poor decision-making by looking at Cain. His point of departure analytically led to murder.

There is a relation between belief system (faith) and perception of risk. Religions that depend on personal works for salvation render a greater fear factor for failure because divine protection is not assured. One the other hand, our biblical foundations do not support a spirit of fear. Belief in Christ takes away the fear of death. From a biblical perspective, fear of God means one need not fear anything else. ***ERGO, even "Terrorism" is served by our diminished faith.***

> *"The hand of the Lord was upon me, and he brought me out by the Spirit of the Lord and set me in the middle of a valley; it was full of dry bones. He led me back and forth among them, and I saw a great many bones on the floor of the valley, bones that were very dry. He asked me, "Son of man, can these bones live?"*[87]

The approach that is presented here requires what Richard J. Foster refers to as the "prayer of conscience" and the "prayer of consciousness."[88] The prayer of conscience is asking the Lord to call to memory sins daily so that one may repent and keep very short accounts with God. Then, having accepted Christ, and repented of sins, the next prayer is for the consciousness. The goal is to see as God sees. This prayer is for our Lord to reveal His will and workings during the course of the day and with regard to the materials and questions we have to address on any given day. Repentance coupled with revelation allows for the clarity of vision needed to recognize and reflect on the truths of God's Word and its application for our daily lives.

***

Describe in writing what you see. (A Problem within the Public Policy Domain)

What are the underlying assumptions of the current policy?

What is the rationale given for acceptance?

What are the elements of current policy that are directly linked to the assumptions?

Who are the major actors that tend to shape the policy?

Are the assumptions consistent across stakeholders?

Are these deemed appropriate?

Are any stakeholders omitted from the policy choice conversation?

Why or how have these choices become acceptable?

Describe in writing what the world sees.

How might alternative assumptions be translated into policy? In other words, what would policy look like if according to the world the "appropriate" assumptions were applied?

What are the chances of acceptance of these assumptions?

Can these obstacles be addressed? How, and in what time frame?

What are the most appropriate criteria for assessing future policy initiatives?

What should be avoided at all cost?

If tradeoffs exist, what is expendable? In what situations?

Who should be held accountable? For what should these individuals be held accountable?

Describe in writing what God would say about what you see based upon the Holy Bible, the Written Word of God.

Concentrate deeply upon the passage or scene of scripture that God calls to mind for you. Concentrate by prayerfully asking questions about all who are present within the scene, and the details concerning the actions that are taking place. Then ask God to reveal to you the meaning for the issue at hand. What should we know about God's view that we may gain from the passage in order to grow closer to Him?

Respond to the message that God has given you through your prayers to Him with the resolve that to devote your thoughts, writing, and all other actions in addition to these scholarly pursuits under the guidance of His Holy Spirit and in the obedience of His written Word, the Holy Bible. REMEMBER: It is critical that you test all ideas on the basis of the Holy Bible. God does not contradict himself. The Holy Bible is the final authoritative source, the litmus test for all ideas.

As you explore the passage in relation to the issue at hand, consider the following policy related questions,

Given current conditions, what are the alternative strategies that are acceptable to God?

How should the alternatives be judged?

What can go wrong?

Who stands to benefit given the acceptance of God's alternatives?

What would be the extent of the benefit?

Will the benefit be to the detriment of any other policy objective?

Will the benefit be different for different people?

Who and how much?

Where should resources be directed?

What about other resources?

Translate what God says in the Holy Bible about what you see into word pictures. Remember, to develop a word picture that the secular mind can understand without losing God's meaning. This is the approach our Lord and Savior Jesus Christ used to communicate Kingdom truths.

Paraphrasing

Substitute synonyms for the words as they appear in the biblical text.

Compare the paraphrase with the biblical text to make sure God's meaning is not lost.

Combine and separate sentences as necessary.

Maintain the logical order of the concepts that God wishes to communicate.

Change the word order of major ideas as needed to best communicate His truth.

Write the word picture in accordance with the richest meaning of the text.

Summarizing

With the help of a concordance and other biblical references, look for related situations in which the biblical principles have been applied.

Identify and isolate the most important ideas of the text as they related to the issue at hand and specify the significance.

Combine these concepts into sentences and paragraphs.

Write the word picture in accordance with the richest meaning of the text

Consistent with the Arthur Stinchcombe in *Constructing Social Theories* make sure that you understand the logic of theory construction and testing. As mentioned earlier, claims are the equivalent of hypotheses.[89]

Develop empirical tests for the theories (competing explanations) for the public policy problem under examination.

Check to make sure that in every respect your analysis is consistent with the Word of God.

Based upon your word picture, develop a profound question for which the only answer is Jesus the Christ. (Specify the implications for the issue at hand.)

God's Word Picture as a Faith-filled Projection of New Circumstance

This is what the Sovereign Lord says to these bones; "I will make breath enter you, and you will come to life. I will attach tendons to you and make flesh come upon you and cover you with skin; I will put breath in you, and you will come to life. Then you will know that I am the Lord." Specifically you want to examine the following elements from a biblically informed mind-set.

Conduct the relevant research. According to the Bardach book entitled, *A Practical Guide for Policy Analysis*, the following eight practical steps are essential in the process.[90] Because this discussion as with other similar policy texts pursues a secular worldview, the information must be recast in terms consistent with the biblical worldview.

- Redefine the problem
- Review the evidence
- Reconstruct the alternative strategies for addressing the policy problem
- Select the criteria
- Project the outcomes
- Confront the trade-offs
- Do biblically sound smart practices research

CHAPTER SEVEN

Acknowledging God in Prodigal Societies Writ Global

"When an evil spirit comes into a man, it goest throughout arid places seeking rest and doesn't find it. Then it says, I will return to the house I left. When it arrives and finds that the house is unoccupied, swept clean and put in order, then it goes and takes seven other spirits more wicked than itself and they go in and live there. And, the final condition is worse than the first."[91]

Matthew 12:43-45, Holy Bible, New Living Translation

WORLDLY *COMPASSION?*

With regard to the immigration controversy, evangelicals boast of assisting those in border areas who are suffering physically from the consequences of their attempts to illegally enter the United States. The assistance is greatly appreciated by those receiving the help. However, there is a pattern of thinking that seems to accompany the services that are offered. It is what I would refer to as "Cheap Grace." What do I mean? Well, there is a sense in which many of the new conventions of evangelicalism are leaning toward a non-biblical approach to life with worldly compassionate rhetoric attached. I liken much of that conversation with the same nuances that suggests that an act like spanking one's unruly child lacks "Grace." Those who would adhere to such thinking also believe that to call an "evil"---"evil"--- is unloving. Indeed, it is the same thinking that suggests that there are many roads to God.

A CONTRARY OPINION

Contrary to the worldly stance of "I'm Okay, You're Okay" ;"All Roads Lead to Rome;" and, anything goes, Jesus says, "He is *the* Way!" There is a plumb line. There is law. Without law grace would be unrecognizable and indeed unnecessary. Christ Jesus, full of Grace, said that He did not come to change the law but to complete it. In the same way, repentance is required for salvation. Salvation graciously offered is the result of a deliberate act of godly compassion. That act of payment for sin that Jesus Christ made is extended graciously *only* to those who are willing to accept Him as Savior. Let me stress this point, acknowledgement of sin resulting in repentance [meaning, change in one's direction---turning away from previous thinking to that which aligns oneself with God's perspective] such that one knows that they are in need of a Savior is prerequisite to salvation.

THE RULE OF LAW

It is not a loving thing to ignore rule of law. The United States is jeopardized by simply seeing the border as a geographical area and not as a point of political identity for the nation---a boundary that distinguishes one nation from another. Such a boundary is not unlike the skin that covers each of our bodies so that we can recognize each other. Seeing the border area with current violations is much like seeing an individual that lacks boundaries. Without boundaries, individuals as well as nations are susceptible to the whims of others, readily available to accept lovingly strange philosophies and as a consequence other (counterfeit) gods. Psalm One warns of naiveté, the failure to discern truth from error. Grace does not excuse, it allows for correction. Grace does not lie in word or deed by suggesting that everything is okay when it isn't. On the contrary, grace exposes the wrong and then offers a way out of wrong behavior. "Neither do I accuse you [to the point of stoning], says Jesus. But, *go* and *Sin No More!*"

THE GRACE OF GOD

The Truth is that God warns us against calling "Evil good and good evil." May we encompass the entire Bible in our thinking? May we exercise biblical grace and not cheapen it? Tough love is of greater value in the long run because it calls for prolonged investment of energy and resources to correct a bad situation. To merely empathize without correction is a very selfish act and is indeed more convenient for those who want merely to patch symptoms rather than heal. Such actions make us feel good. However, these superficial actions do not offer a lasting solution. This misnamed "grace" which is merely giving humanitarianism as if humanitarianism is the equivalent to the Gospel of Jesus Christ is problematic. To give assistance without giving the Full Gospel of Jesus Christ is an anemic move on the part of the body of Christ. I repeat. Let us not be confused by thinking that the Gospel of Jesus Christ is correctly portrayed simply by offering assistance in the form of services or deliverables. The Gospel is not social services delivery as well meaning as such Samaritan help may be. Rather, the Gospel of Jesus Christ more profoundly offers spiritual deliverance---a change that eliminates the need for chains on the demoniac or even a fence around a nation. The spiritual deliverance needed is from the entrapment associated with living in the kingdom of darkness rather than the kingdom of light. What would Jesus do in the case of illegal entry into the nation? He would say, "Go and Sin No More."

THE GOOD NEWS!

The bad news is that all of us are sinners. And, that is why the Good News is Good News! The gracious Good News is that Christ Jesus died for our sins. He paid a high price so that we now can choose to rightly align ourselves with Him in the power of His Holy Spirit. Christ died so that we can live in Him, victoriously rightly reconciled with the Great Law Giver, God, the Sovereign of the universe from which the concept of sovereignty was embraced by the founders of our nation.

One of the great paradoxes of the church is that when the church is persecuted, the message of the gospel of Jesus Christ is clear. When the church is socially accepted, the message of the gospel becomes obscured.[92] The era following Constantine is the prime example in history. Yet, there is increased acceptability of "faith based initiatives" that incorporate the use of church and para-church operations into the functional arm of government as direct providers of social services to the public. In recent years, this notion of the efficacy of "faith based" service provision has been challenged. The most recent accounts have pointed to the results that many "faith related agencies are loosely tied to faith in terms of resources, more tightly coupled in terms of authority, and moderately coupled with respect to culture; that certain aspects of service-delivery technology are heavily secularized in many agencies.[93]

Several scholars who have explored the dynamics of such coupling have suggested beneficial implications of the secular to faith-based agency linkage. However, according to Smith and Sosin, 2001, "... agencies have varying ties to religion, and these ties affect the agencies' organization moderately to profoundly"; "... that there is no easy or simple trade-off between the extent to which an agency expresses faith and its size, use of secular resources, or similar factors"; and, ultimately, "... many of the statements about 'faith-based' agencies that are made in the popular press or by politicians are overly simplistic; arguments in favor of faith-based service delivery are mismatched with the true universe of religiously tied agencies and their characteristics. In other words, the vision of agencies that is stated by many contemporary policy makers and presidential candidates represents only a small percentage of the total spectrum of agencies that have an important faith component."[94] Often overlooked in this discussion are the implications of such linkages for the original mission of the church, the spreading of the gospel. Further, it may be contended that in an age of increased globalization and social conflict directly associated with race, ethnicity, and religion, that the merits of "faith" as a means of organizing and distributing services within this society should be reassessed. This book attempts to synthesize the various elements in the development of a theoretical perspective on the conflicting roles of the church as provider of social services delivery in contrast to provider of spiritual deliverance in secular society, the principle components presented through the formulation of several propositions which link social service delivery via the "church" to social distance between ethnic, racial and religious groups. By coupling, what is referred to is the linkage between secular governmental or nongovernmental intermediary agencies and the faith-based organization. Coupling is an indicator of the social acceptability of the religious entity. Coupling can take a variety of forms and degrees of intensity. Coupling can take the form of resource dependency; organizational authority, and organizational culture. The coupling can be minimal, having an insignificant impact on the religious identity and mandate of the organization that is providing the services under the auspices of the church. Or, the coupling can be extreme, where the governing authorities outside of the church have ultimate say concerning the operation of the organization, and indeed, the organization learns secular culture. If the impact of socially acceptable church is the obscuring the gospel, as more enter the church looking for the spiritual truth, they many not find it. In fact, what is offered especially with the coupling of the church to secular funding of social service delivery is a maintenance-based social mechanism, designed primarily for the absorption of social tension. There are political implications for the mission of the church.[95]

TAKE NO BRIBES AGAINST THE INNOCENT!

The Church must not fumble in its responsibility of passing on the gospel of Jesus Christ. The Church is to supply to society salt and light by the lives of individuals that make up the Church and not the institution itself.

The spiritual issues for which Christ is given as a prescription from God lose priority of focus in the broadening acceptability of "faith initiatives" to address societal ills. In secular service delivery coupling there is the obscuring of preaching of the gospel. There is the casting of societal issues in terms of demographic characteristic and to do so by means of religious rhetorical device sends the wrong message to the lost. Therefore the distinction between religion and race becomes obscured because the religion of this age is secular humanism, a religion replete with demographic imagery.

The whole task of research is to acquire knowledge. And, the process of understanding is made up of a myriad of decisions. These decisions include:

- The decision to observe a phenomenon or phenomena

- The decision involving the development of plausible explanations for what has been observed
- The decision to devise appropriate tests of the alternative theories
- The decisions concerning the appropriate interpretation of what is discovered
- The decisions exploring the amount of risk associated with acceptance of the interpretations; and,
- The decisions concerning whether one has observed enough.

Accompanying these decisions are strategies of inquiry. The scientific method provides a basic framework for inquiry relying upon specific stages. First, observation can be susceptible to a number of problems not the least of which is the bias of interpretation. But, in addition there are potential problems of desensitization, and the general acceptance of prevailing assumptions, the acceptance of which precludes the "need" to look further at a phenomenon. The second stage is explanation. Here, the goal is identify all the possible reasons why the phenomenon you see exists. What can go wrong at this stage of trying "to know" something includes the failure to identify plausible alternatives. Also, there is the possible failure to move beyond conventional operational and conceptual definitions of variables to employ other possibilities. How one defines what is being observed has an impact upon what one finds. The third stage in the process of inquiry is the test. This is the procedure that one develops to determine the credibility of the explanations offered to explain the existence of the observed phenomenon. It is the testing process that is the primary concern of this primer. Tests may stem from either inductive or deductive. Inductive reasoning is based upon the cumulative evidence that once pieced together leads to a generalization that summarizes that evidence. Deductive reasoning stresses the move from the general to the specific. The idea is that if a specific statement is true, then one would expect to find evidence that is consistent with the statement in a variety of settings.

Example of Equi-finality

The example is rural policy implementation strategies and their accompanying results. The stated goal has been to reduce the amount of poverty experienced in a Midwestern state. What follows is a brief description of the structural/functional characteristics of administrative networks that supply unemployment and related support services in the various communities.[96]

It has been argued that S maintains H where,

H = level of rural poor in a selected state

S = structure (economic and accompanying support services) contributing to maintenance of the level of rural poverty

T = upsetting tensions (i.e., corporate openings, call backs, positive economic turnarounds, and migratory influxes)

The claim is that when T increases, H is not naturally maintained.

This description paints the picture that there are artificially contrived limits above and below which will not be exceeded due to the presence of S.

Example of Self-Replicating Loops

Rural poverty example again! The variables would be as follows:

K = capacity of groups to impact S (structures)

C = the effect of maintaining H (Poor) on each group = consequence

R = proportional effect of T (Tensions) on H

So, what difference does intervention make domestically and internationally? This is the question the evaluation of public policy impact and programmatic operation is designed to answer. However, before measurement of impact is pursued, potential pitfalls must be avoided. Those in decision making positions should:

- ---Avoid *equi-finality*---the most obvious sign of the presence of equi-finality is the policy discourse that suggests much activity automatically equates to addressing the defined problem.[97]

- ---Be aware of periphery activity in which much is going on but little is being accomplished because the focus of the activity misses the mark.

- ---Be weary of mutual admiration activities where participants and identified stakeholders feel good about each others' activity while the activity itself fails to bear fruit for the public

- ---Avoid the "Too little, too late" syndrome that represents allocation of insufficient resources and time to accomplish what is required to be successful.

- ---Avoid successfully solving the wrong problem. This still represents a policy failure because the problem for which the initiative was mandated has not been solved.

- ---Avoid the popular misinterpretation that allocation of resources automatically means problem resolution, and finally,

- ---Avoid the misspecification of benefit due to the nature of beneficiaries. (An example would include impoverished persons who may be perceived as "undeserving poor."

Evaluation Methodology and Use

In the discussion of explanation, decision research, judgmental aspects, the detriment(s) cause consequence, **Y**, therefore X1, X2,..., Xn should be elements that may be manipulated to address problem outcome Y. The question of the relation between policy and causality deserves exploration.

Explanation for the existence of phenomenon dictates specific action for its resolution or amelioration. To explain why a problem exists presumes first that the problem has been defined both conceptually and operationally such that a consensus has been developed about the nature of the problem. Competing definitions of the problem lead to competing views about its resolution. The definition of the problem that becomes the problem on which action is taken is made so because of the legitimacy of the offered description. One author has described "legitimacy" as being tantamount to "defining reality to others." The definition aspect is critical.

Pitfalls experienced in theory that lead to poor policy would include the problem of fallacy and related maladies in the use of rhetoric when basic policy questions are cast. But, perhaps and even more critical dilemma is that posed by the prevalence of confusing description with explanation. Description is defined by Webster as, "the act of describing; specifically, the discourse intended to give a mental image of something to discuss "what" contributed to the existence of that thing. We appear to be captivated by demographic imagery that allows us to describe the characteristics of those experiencing various social problems without actually addressing root cause. Policy fails in large part because true causality remains outside the realm of policy discourse. As a consequence, such incomplete assessments, although often well-meaning, render faulty explanations, the direct result of lies of omission. It is as if the process has too many iterative steps to move the public and its officials to that level of inquiry.[98] And, when causality is discussed, it is usually left to those policy issues that are limited in potential impact on society. The worst case scenario, however, is the explanation when the explanation that is offered is erroneous.

Misspecification of the cause during problem definition has potentially adverse ramifications, often leading to policies that not only fail to ameliorate the problem but, worse yet, contribute to the existence of other problems. Indeed, a spiral may evolve from the point of misspecification of problem and to the development of institutions and actions that exhaust both resources and time. Huntington[99], although in another vein, etc. talks about the development of institutions and the potential impact of these mechanisms for securing political stability. There are routes for venting frustration when the social problem occurs. The institutions are there in essence to absorb tension and to reroute and even defuse energy that may be disruptive to the system of things. Huntington discusses the vulnerable periods, that is, the time and circumstances that persons are most apt to be disruptive because some apparent discrepancy in the perception of what is and "what should be." The lesson learned here is first, that problem definition is not inconsequential to public policy development. The definition that is prescribed determines action. And, the nature of the action taken is further determined by the perceived causal relation between the existence of the problem as defined and the presence of factors that lead to the existence of the problem. Later, in the chapter on evaluation, we will discuss how causal explanation works in the development of criteria of performance in the execution of policy.

How progress should be measured in response to key arguments? What does this mean in terms of the secular environment; biblically framed initiatives; multiculturalism; invasion of other gods; policy agendas in prodigal societies? In response to these questions, consider:

-Incidences where societal estimations and declared problem definition that proceeds without benefit of the moral clarity that comes from right acknowledgement of God, possess seeds of futility.

The challenge is to explore the implications of strategic decision-making in the direction of governance that has its point of departure the acknowledgement of God. Consider an alternative approach to assessing public policy issues that incorporates the tools needed for testing the truthfulness of explanation upon which future action may rest. It is even more important to offer a biblically informed approach to public policy decision making so that God may be rightly acknowledge in the making of decisions of state. And, in the international arena, remember God's Word concerning Israel.

GOD'S VIEW OF ISRAEL

Ezekiel 36

God says,

> *"Son of man, prophesy to the mountains of Israel and say, 'O mountains of Israel, hear the word of the LORD. This is what the Sovereign LORD says: The enemy said of you, "Aha! The ancient heights have become our possession."' Therefore prophesy and say, "This is what the Sovereign LORD says: Because they ravaged and hounded you from every side so that you became the possession of the rest of the nations and the object of people's malicious talk and slander, therefore, O mountains of Israel, hear the word of the Sovereign LORD: This is what the Sovereign LORD says to the mountains and hills, to the ravines and*

valleys, to the desolate ruins and the deserted towns that have been plundered and ridiculed by the rest of the nations around you---this is what the Sovereign LORD says: In my burning zeal I have spoken against the rest of the nations, and against all Edom, for with glee and with malice in their hearts they made my land their own possession so that they might plunder its pastureland,' Therefore prophesy concerning the land of Israel and say to the mountains and hills, to the ravines and valleys: "This is what the Sovereign LORD says: I speak in my jealous wrath because you have suffered the scorn of the nations. Therefore this is what the Sovereign LORD says: I swear with uplifted hand that the nations around you will also suffer scorn.

"But you, O mountains of Israel, will produce branches and fruit for my people Israel, for they will soon come home. I am concerned for you and will look on you with favor; you will be plowed and sown, and I will multiply the number of people upon you, even the whole house of Israel. The towns will be inhabited and the ruins rebuilt. I will increase the number of men and animals upon you, and they will be fruitful and become numerous. I will settle people on you as in the past and will make you prosper more than before. Then you will know that I am the LORD. I will cause people, my people Israel, to walk upon you. They will possess you, and you will be their inheritance; you will never again deprive them of their children.

"'This is what the Sovereign LORD says: Because people say to you, "You devour men and deprive your nation of its children," therefore you will no longer devour men or make your nation childless, declares the Sovereign LORD. No longer will you suffer the scorn of the peoples or cause your nation to fall, declares the Sovereign LORD.'"

Again the word of the LORD came to me: "Son of man, when the people of Israel were living in their own land, they defiled it by their conduct and their actions. Their conduct was like a woman's monthly uncleanness in my sight. So I poured out my wrath on them because they had shed blood in the land and because they had defiled it with their idols. I dispersed them among the nations, and they were scattered through the countries; I judged them according to their conduct and their actions. And wherever they went among the nations they profaned my holy name, for it was said of them, "These are the LORD's people, and yet they had to leave his land.' I had concern for my holy name, which the house of Israel profaned among the nations where they had gone.

"Therefore say to the house of Israel, ' This is what the Sovereign LORD says: It is not for your sake, O house of Israel, that I am going to do these things, but for the sake of my holy name which you have profaned among the nations where you have gone. I will show the holiness of my great name, which has been profaned among the nations, the name you have profaned among the nations, the name you have profaned among them. Then the nations will know that I am the LORD, declares the Sovereign LORD, when I show myself holy through you before their eyes.

"'For I will take you out of the nations; I will gather you from all the countries and bring you back into your own land. I will sprinkle clean water on you, and you will be clean; I will cleanse you from all your impurities and from all your

idols. I will give you a new heart and put a new sprit in you; I will remove from you your heart of stone and give you a heart of flesh. And I will put my Spirit in you and move you to follow my decrees and be careful to keep my laws. You will live in the land I gave your forefathers; you will be my people, and I will be your God. I will save you from all your uncleanness. I will call for the grain and make it plentiful and will not bring famine upon you. I will increase the fruit of the trees and the crops of the field, so that you will jo longer suffer disgrace among the nations because of famine. Then you will remember your evil ways and wicked deeds, and you will loathe yourselves for your sins and detestable practices. I want you to know that I am not doing this for your sake, declares the Sovereign LORD. Be ashamed and disgraced for your conduct, O house of Israel!

"'This is what the Sovereign LORD says: On the day I cleanse you from all your sins, I will resettle your towns, and the ruins will be rebuilt. The desolate land will be cultivated instead of lying desolate in the sight of all who pass through it. They will say, "This land that was laid waste has become like the Garden of Eden; the cities that were lying in ruins, desolate ad destroyed, are now fortified and inhabited." Then the nations around you that remain will know that I, the LORD, have rebuilt what was destroyed and have replanted what was desolate. I, the LORD, have spoken, and I will do it.'

"This is what the Sovereign LORD says: One again I will yield to the plea of the house of Israel and do this for them: I will make their people as numerous as sheep, as numerous as the flocks for offerings at Jerusalem during her appointed feasts. So will the ruined cities be filled with flock of people. Then they will know that I am the LORD."[100]

God plans to judge all of the nations on earth with regard to their treatment of Israel.

POINTS TO REMEMBER:

1. Derivative thought is thought that starts from a fragmented element of the Truth and progresses without benefit of discernment.

2. Derivative thought results in government policy spirals responsible for large expenditure of resources that contribute to deficit spending.

3. And, because the solution strategies miss the mark, the results at best are temporarily beneficial, contradictory, and unstable for the society to move forward.

4. This problem of derivative thought is keen in the developed world and is the primary obstacle to nation building in the less developed world.

5. The problem of derivative thought is the first stage toward wicked reasoning.

6. Wicked reasoning (twisted not unlike wicker furniture) twists reality into capsule sized renditions of fragmented truths that lead to circular reasoning.

7.

Areas of governance that would benefit from another view, but this time from a biblically informed perspective may be found in Table 7.1 below.

TABLE 7.1

RECOMMENDED SERIES OF ROUNDTABLE THEMES

LAW
-Natural Law as the basis for Establishing
International Norms
-Territorial Disputes
-Monitoring the Implementation of International
  Covenants
-Terrorism and Counter Terrorism &
International Law
-International Religious Freedom Act

TRADE
-Justice and International Trade
-Economic Globalization
-Investment Relations in Security Strategies
-International Trafficking
-International Terrorism & Market
-International Divisions of Labor
-Poor Populations
-Peacekeeping and International Economy
-Economic Strategies for National Security

TECHNOLOGY
-Anti-Terrorism Measures
-International Development Management
-International Imagery (Media)
-Environmental Security
-Eco-Violence
-Macro/Micro Criminology
-Third World Security Issues

ETHICS
-Role of Nongovernmental Organizations in
International Security
-Transnational NGO Dynamics
-Moral Agency and International Security
-International Business Ethics
-Buildings Dedicated to Religious Activity
-Ethnic Relations
-Transnational Criminal Activity and Ethical
Governance

DEMOGRAPHY & SOCIO-POLITICAL
SUPPORT SYSTEMS
-Demographic Aspects of International Order
-Conflict Management: International Norms
about Individual and Group Rights (Ethnic
Identity)
-Regional International Relations
-Ecological Crisis & Food Security
-Humanitarian Intervention
-Combination of Religion & Culture
-Profiling as a Security Measure
-Differential Demographics—The Case of Israel
-Urbanization and Security
-Human Rights
-Gender & Sexuality
-Women and Children
-Redemption of Failed States
-Religion in Post Communist Societies
-Identity Politics and International Security
-Religion and Democratic

ACTION POINT

Let us assume that your observation is that we have seen a change in the degree of U.S. foreign policy support granted Israel. More specifically – the degree of visible support for continued nationhood. Evidence of erosion might be indicated by:

Territorial boundary erosion – measured in square miles; caliber of lands taken; or a combination of those factors;

Toleration for Israeli vulnerability – measured in the number of attacks that are directly attributable to increased vulnerability given changed borders;

Changed alliance Mid-East nations – measured by the increased number of meetings for negotiation with international stakeholders that have openly declared a desire for increased reduction of Israeli territory.

Changed alliance global – measured by the number of votes by the United States in the UN siding with the international stakeholders that the U.S. has not sided with in the recent past.

Possible explanation(s) – [Explanation is theory]

Theory 1: The change in support for Israel is due to U.S. budgetary constraints. Budgetary Constraints measured in terms of % change in allocated US military expenditures allocated to Israeli support.

Theory 2: Increased military commitment to other trouble spots in the world. Military commitment measured as the change in # of diverse locations military forces have been deployed within a specified timeframe.

Theory 3: Shift in degree of global interdependency for the protection of US interests abroad. Global interdependency measured as the change in # of unilateral interventions compared to total # of military engagements the US has undertaken within a specified period of time.

Such that,

Global Interdependency = # of unilateral interventions/total # of military engagements

Do you see a pattern to the above? The pattern of thinking is this:

- Observation [in general terms]
- Evidence of Observation [measurable indicators]
- Explanations (meaning Theories) in general terms
- Evidence of the credibility of the theory(ies) in measurable terms
- Such that one can see if there is a co-relations between the presence of what you see and the measures that would be associated with your theory (explanation).

Now, you try it.

What Do You See?

The Art of Observation

- What do you see?
- Is there a problem?
- What makes what you see problematic?
- What is possibly causing that problem? (Identify alternative explanations-theories)
- Define the causes of the problem.
- What would be evidence that the problem is getting worse?

Write the policy position by telling the whole story. [101]

The following is a general example of how you might framework thoughts:

Paragraph Set #1

Statement of what has been done so far. (Literature Review)

Statement about what has been learned, summarized in one sentence.

Statement: "If this is true, the following conclusions are relevant to our current situation."

Paragraph Set #2

The initial or simple answer is as follows...

But, there are complexities that keep us from operating upon that answer.

The situation is more like… (Word Picture Inserted Here)

Therefore, a more realistic definition of the problem given the complexities is as follows…

The implications of this more complex definition are…

Paragraph Set #3

And, if the nature of the real problem is X, then aspects of the problem may be documented further as can seen in the case of…

Insert a qualifier narrowing the discussion to one population while describing applicability for other populations, settings, or other units of analysis.

The requirements are…

But the reality is…

And even though the impression is…

The reality is…

Until Y, there will be a discrepancy that impinges upon an aspect of X.

The same pattern can be seen in other cases such as…

In the above situation, the impact was some aspect of X.

And this phenomenon supports the impression of some Y that is not true.

When this is coupled with other things (specify A, B, C, Z here) a negative consequence results.

Contemporary thinking has it that…

But the general public has not been able to see it because of the mechanisms (specify imagery) that support erroneous view.

Examples of mechanism(s) support the erroneous view.

Example of where it does not work.

The impact of the absence of the erroneous view is…

How people who are where the erroneous view does not exist view the place where it does. The acceptance of the erroneous view or myth about the others…

How the people who are where the erroneous view does not exist view the place where it does. The acceptance of the erroneous view or myth about the others…

Paragraph Set #4

A given consequence of x leads to other difficulties.

Difficulty 1, 2, n (Specify all)

Because of a certain action, the following has happened.

Specific examples include...

An application...

The implication...

The translation of one activity into meaning something else...

No matter how positive the reaction, the controlling factor is B

B is typically absent in our situation.

The [stakeholder(s) specified here] do not see the translated situation.

The see it as...

The consequence of this activity based upon the stakeholder(s) operative premise has been...

Paragraph Set #5

Due to disparity, the following consequence has resulted.

The problem here, in the current or proposed strategy is...

An alternative is proposed because...

Otherwise the consequence is/will be...

Then, to the original listed above problems are/will be added complexities that result from...

The innovation offered has consequences for all aspects of...

This tactic/strategy/alternative will give the stakeholder(s) what they want (specify) with the least adversity/cost or maximum benefit given current or future constraints.

CHAPTER EIGHT

Acknowledging God in Measuring Progress

The Logic of Public Policy Evaluation

The logic of evaluation of public policy and its subsequent programs from a practical or formative perspective linking methodological techniques to the question of operational efficiency, effectiveness, and the summative impact is the approach to analysis to be taken here. This approach relies upon the following major steps: (i) the statement of goals, objectives, sub-objectives and tasks; (ii) the examination of factors required for the achievement of specified outcomes; (iii) the relative weight associated with the highest probability of success compared to the amount that is actually exhibited; and (iv) the impact of the combined activity has on the population requiring the services being rendered.

The statement of goals and objectives is theory based. The idea is to specify in measurable terms what the goal is. Then, one must review the literature and other means of information collection to determining what contributes to the presence or prohibits the presence of the desired goal. Once this is done, each of the factors mentioned will be assessed to determine if they elements may be manipulated. If they can, then they may become a component of the operation (assuming the operation is not currently in existence). If there are factors that cannot be manipulated, then the goal will be to identify those actions required to minimize the negative impact of adverse factors present. All factors of significant import must be addressed to improve the probability of success. If there are limited resources available, then choices must be made about what should be included. Those factors carrying the greatest amount of weight of explanatory power should be addressed, with only minor factors included when they are critical to the sequences required for the success of the more powerful indicators.

Measuring Success

What is implied is a photo of conditions past and present that allows one to determine what difference an intervention has made. The snapshot can be as simple as an indicator or as complex as an index for which we are concerned about current and past status. The measure of difference made is impossible without a counterfactual, a statement of what would have been if no intervention had taken place.

The act of seeing is strategic in this process. Here, what we are doing is "seeing" something that deserves an explanation. Of course, an explanation without an observation is backward. And, although noted political scientists and policy analysts have remarked that politicians have solutions for which they seek problems – that should not be the goal of applied policy research. That especially should not be the case for policy and program evaluation.

What is policy and program evaluation? It is the applied research designed to determine the level of effectiveness and/or efficiency of public sector initiatives. More specifically, policy evaluators answer questions concerning the impact of decisions made by public sector and related actors. Program evaluators answer execution questions like "How well is an organizational arm of a given policy functioning?" This may be in terms of process of implementation of initiatives, the actual installation of a program. Or, it may entail the determination of overall impact of one or a series of activities that were begun with a specified set of goals and objectives in mind. The programs themselves (if designed appropriately) will have an organizational strategy that may allow us to identify the organizational elements whose specific tasks are needed to address the social problem at hand. Indeed, recent evaluation literature stresses the need for the use of theory-driven approaches to both the development of initiatives and the assessment of those activities.

The process of evaluation stresses *(i)* a recognized theoretical relation between the presence of a desired outcome and the nature of the intervention; *(ii)* the presence of a program intervention that has an anticipated effect; *(iii)* the presence of a counterfactual; and *(iv)* a recognized method for determining the extent to which the desired effect was realized.

Theory-driven approaches to evaluation require that the determinants of a desired outcome be identified. Literature over the social phenomenon to be addressed will discuss cause and effect. The goal is to develop implementation apparatus with this information in mind. And, perhaps more importantly, given this knowledge of the relationship, operations should be designed to provide those determinants. The departure from social science comes with the emphasis upon those variables that are administratively within one's control. So policy emphasis is upon those X's that are manipulated. It is these variables that become the point of focus for program development.

This is the Initial Checklist to consider when describing the attributes of an organization (or the implementation apparatus) that may have implications for program effectiveness:

1. The mandate of the entity

2. Source of staff

3. Planning body that endorsed the establishment of the organization

4. Political and nonpolitical actors that have an influence on the organization's existence and network clout---Board of Directors, Advisors--- source/backgrounds---benefit

5. Organizational chart(s)---or description of staff configuration

6. Decision points---routine vs. non-routine in a centralized versus decentralized

7. External factors that influence the direction of the organization

8. Internal factors that influence the direction of the organization

9. Budget Allocation/Financial Sources

10. History of the functions performed---the historical progression of increased (or declining) responsibilities/functions and accompanying rationale

11. Characteristics of dissolution of subparts of the organization or specific functions

12. Latitude and longevity of parts of the organization in relation to geographical context

13. Condition of subparts of the organization

14. Diversity of functions performed within subparts of the organization

15. New functions are added under what conditions?

16. Characteristics of plans for development of the entity currently

17. Planned development in relation to government/political processes in decision-making

18. Perceived objectives

19. Perceived success

20. How success is measured by that entity

Given the presences of a theoretical relation between programmatic strategy and outcome, the evaluation criteria for acceptable programmatic performance may be established. This measure is contingent upon appropriate implementation of the programmatic design. The criteria may be established given the expected outcome parameters. Quality control measures may be instituted when it comes to formative evaluation. With regard to the summative or "impact" evaluation, the issue of expected versus actual result becomes more sophisticated. It may require any one or combination of techniques such as randomized experiments or designs relying heavily upon regression related techniques.

Measuring success involves more than the quality of service delivered, it also requires measuring the extent to which the initiative that is implemented addresses the demand. It is possible to be 100% successful with a program or initiative for which only 20% of the need is addressed. This consequence needs to be recognized when such limited coverage of the problem exists in order that a complete picture of the status of things may be depicted.

Public policy may be viewed from a perspective other than the public policy process. Public policy may be viewed from the standpoint of institutions in which human analogy is offered as another way of understanding organizations.[102] For example, Guy Peters describes the organization's fiscal posture at times as "gluttonous" when they consume many funds; and, as constipated when they fail to produce. In Peter's discussion of policy dynamics, lineage of organization, "begetting" organizations appear. There is even a discussion of the life cycle of organizations moving from gestation with the development of a policy mandate toward maturity and death. Institutions then become a frame of reference for the discussion of policy recommendations and choices. Current status of that discussion seems to center on issue domains and how institutions are to cope with change.

Figure 8.1

The Big Picture with Corresponding Methods

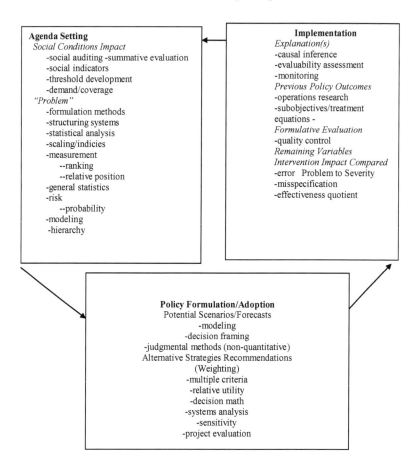

Agenda Setting
Social Conditions Impact
   -social auditing -summative evaluation
   -social indicators
   -threshold development
   -demand/coverage
"Problem"
   -formulation methods
   -structuring systems
   -statistical analysis
   -scaling/indicies
   -measurement
     --ranking
     --relative position
   -general statistics
   -risk
     --probability
   -modeling
   -hierarchy

Implementation
Explanation(s)
-causal inference
-evaluability assessment
-monitoring
Previous Policy Outcomes
-operations research
-subobjectives/treatment
equations -
Formulative Evaluation
-quality control
Remaining Variables
Intervention Impact Compared
-error Problem to Severity
-misspecification
-effectiveness quotient

Policy Formulation/Adoption
Potential Scenarios/Forecasts
-modeling
-decision framing
-judgmental methods (non-quantitative)
Alternative Strategies Recommendations
(Weighting)
-multiple criteria
-relative utility
-decision math
-systems analysis
-sensitivity
-project evaluation

From the standpoint of deterministic models that stress cause and effect (causal theory) we need only review the arguments that are presented to endorse or rebuke choice in the policy system. By policy system, we are referring to what William Dunn maintains as "The overall institutional pattern within which policies are made."[103] According to Dunn, "Three elements of a policy system are public policies, policy stakeholders, and policy environments."[104] Specific examples for the use of these models rest with argument initially. Then, deterministic models are applied to forecasting methods used "... to produce information about the probably consequences of future courses of action. Finally, in the development of both the monitoring and evaluation strategies takes place at those stages of information about past causes and consequences of policies,"[105] Further, evaluation consists of a collection of methods used, "to produce information about the value or worth of organizational activities."[106]

Governments, International and Domestic Nongovernmental Organization and Other Private Sector Policy Narratives and Social Conditions

The question of the relation between policy and causality deserves exploration. The explanation of the existence of phenomenon dictates specific action for its resolution or amelioration. To explain why a problem exists presumes first that the problem has been defined both conceptually and operationally, and a consensus has been developed about the nature of the problem. Competing definitions of the problem lead to competing views about its resolution. The rejected definition is acted on because of the legitimacy of the offered description.

Coleman elaborates the benefits associated with the use of propositions and their statement in mathematical terms.[107] With that idea in mind, but cast in terms of policy inputs and outputs, at each state of the policy making process, evaluation in a generic sense can take place. Starting with needs assessment, a series of questions may be addressed. As a consequence of the use of a myriad of possible data collection strategies, the evaluative question is "What needs to be done?" or "What problem exists?" can be answered. Identification of problem meriting policy response followed by a decision about what appropriate response should entail, leads to the need for an examination of policy execution often referred to as implementation analysis. Implementation studies are employed to determine whether the program(s) have been executed according to planned design. This is important for purposes of accountability and compliance, but it is also important from a research standpoint of theory driven response to problems and the generalizability of policy results.

By theory-driven response, we are referring to the match between what has been identified as the decided cause of the problem and those activities that will address the cause. We need to know: Can we actually attribute the change that occurs to the implemented policy? If the program is initiated to determine the potential impact the policy strategy may have on a problem, the public sector may attempt a prototype strategy. Such inquiry may take the form of randomized experiments with the evaluative question being, "Can a desired outcome be attributed to the presence of a specified intervention?" In this controlled setting, the treatment may be allotted on the basis of change.

Because of the political nature of service provision and/or regulation, other strategies may be employed to determine potential impact of intervention. Among these strategies are regression discontinuity which answers the question, "How much benefit is actually gleaned from exposure to the program by a limited number of the pool qualified to receive the intervention?" There is the randomized comparative change (RCC) strategy which allows the comparison of groups that have same levels of exposure to problems but a randomized few actually receive the intervention. The question answered by RCC is given a point of in comparison with similar cases, how much changed status may be attributed to intervention? Nonequivalent Control Group Design (NCGD) answers the question, "Is there a significant difference between pre and post-test? Interrupted Time Series Design (ITS) answers the question, How much change in trend status of a phenomenon may be attributed to intervention? IN addition, there are retrospective and futuristic strategies. These include the Post-Only Correlation Design (POC), this respectively answers the question, "What is the relationship between the degree of exposure to a treatment and the value of a desired outcome?" Benefit/Cost Analysis (BCA) addresses the question, "Is the amount of benefit derived worth the cost of intervention when compared to other possible alternatives?" Multi-attribute Evaluation (MEA) answers the question, "How do stakeholders perceive the

performance of the intervention; and what risks are tolerable?" The Sub-objective Design
focuses on the implementation design strategy by answering the question, "What is the nature
of the relation between intervention, sub-objectives and the outcome?" And, it is with this
very practical question the evaluation becomes centered because all of the strategies that are
employed are done to answer one overarching question, "What difference did or will policy
intervention make?" The difference the policy will make is a policy evaluation question. The
focus is on estimating futuristically by measuring retrospectively the change that has
occurred. The goal in this new millennium is to avoid the policy spiral described earlier.

Given the presence of a theoretical relation between programmatic strategy and
outcome, the evaluation criteria for acceptable programmatic performance may be
established. This measure is contingent upon appropriate implementation of the
programmatic design. The criteria may be established given the expected outcome
parameters. Quality control measures may be instituted when it comes to formative
evaluation. With regard to the summative or "impact" evaluation, the issue of expected
versus actual result becomes more sophisticated. It may require any one or combination of
techniques such as randomized experiments or designs relying heavily upon regression
techniques.

Measuring success involves more than the quality of service delivered, it also requires
measuring the extent to which the initiative that is implemented addresses the demand. It is
possible to be 100% successful with a program or initiative for which only 20% of the need
addressed. This consequence needs to be recognized when such limited coverage of the
problem exists in order that a complete picture of the status things may be depicted.

From the standpoint of deterministic models that stress cause and effect (causal theory)
we need only review the arguments that are presented to endorse or rebuke choice in the
policy system. By policy system, we are referring to what Dunn maintains as "the overall
institution pattern within which policies are made." According to Dunn, "The three elements
of a policy system are public policies, policy stakeholders, and policy environments."[108]
Specific examples of the use of these models rest with argument initially. Then, deterministic
models are applied to forecasting methods used "to produce information about the probably
consequences of future courses of action." Finally, in the development of both the monitoring
and evaluation strategies at those states of the public policy process, monitoring is defined as

a collection of methods designed, to produce information about the past causes and consequences of policies."[109] Further, evaluation consists of a collection of methods used, "to produce information about the value of worth of organizational activities."

Political science has contributed the discussion of political feasibility, administrative feasibility, public participation, predictability, procedural due process, international relations, and, reform of government institutions. In essence, theirs is a discussion of power to enact and carry out policy rather than decision making in the formulation.

Hogwood and Gunn maintain that public policy is distinguishable from decision because it encompasses a number of decisions. It requires an examination of pre- and post decisions. And, these authors maintain that public policy goes beyond the decision maker to a myriad of stakeholders and actors. Policy is more closely paralleled to administration. Because of the aggregative nature of policy, public policy analysis takes a variety of forms: i) policy content studies; ii) policy process studies; iii) studies of policy output; iv) evaluation; v) information for policy making; vi) process advocacy; vii) analysis of analysis, or meta analysis.[110]

Correspondingly, Hogwood and Gunn maintain that policy may be viewed from the following perspective: i) field of activity; ii) as an "expression of general purpose" of desired state of affairs; iii) as specific proposals; iv) as a program package; vii) as output form government; viii) as outcome achievement; ix) as a theory or model (implied cause and effect); and, x) as process.[111]

Does the mechanism of policy analysis standup to challenges of the thinking needed to address problems potentially affecting the public? How will we determine what is problematic? Who will we consider the public? These are primordial questions that must be considered. The technical methods often employed by policy analysts have as their roots a combination of social science methodology and quantitative techniques borrowed from the fields of economic business.

Focusing on specific issues presents the possibility for comparative analysis of initiatives. Another view is offered here. It is imperative that we approach public policy as tools for improvement of life. That means the initiatives take on functional purpose. It also means that inquiry associated with public policy will go beyond science for science sake to that of societal construction for which explanation, projection, and amelioration become primary goals of inquiry. The dominant questions with regard to amelioration of problems then become:

What constitutes a problem?

What are the degrees or gradients of severity associated with the problem?

What constitutes progress?

When is a problem no longer a problem?

What are the implications of the existence of the problem in the midst of globalization?

Are there competing assumptions about the nature of the problem and/or the policy response?

These are difficult yet unavoidable questions. The logic of evaluation is applied to the policy and programmatic response society gives to "problems". The evaluative questions are less broad but are no less shaped ultimately by normative responses to the above questions. They have to do with issues of accountability, discrepancy, change and collaboration. The accountability orientation entails the itemization of objectives of operation at all levels of program execution. It requires the determination of prerequisites for optimal operation and the development and subsequent measure of absolute standards of efficiency and effectiveness. The accountability measured is that of decision-makers and designees at various operational levels of the organization. The product of this activity would be the structural and functional characteristics of the operation under review; factors determining the direction in which the entity is evolving; and the degree to which the operative entity has been able to reach implied and specifically mandated goals/objectives as well as those set operationally by the decision-maker. The evaluation process follows the above from a discrepancy orientation – that is, to what degree does actual deviate from plan in relation to:

- Design of organization versus actual operation;
- Expected versus observed performance

Planned versus observed linkages between functional entities within and between organizations are required to work collaboratively in the achievement of specified goals. To measure discrepancy the issue of accountability is ever present in

- The itemization of objectives at all operational levels
- Determination of the prerequisites of the operation; and
- The development and measure of absolute standards of efficiency and effectiveness.

To the extent that the operation is multi-channeled for change, a case where many activities or operations are underway to achieve aspects of the same goal, it is necessary to determine the comprehensive nature of the initiative. This involves determining if the initiative is

- Shaped by pre-existing structure/function characteristics;
- To what degree is consolidation, dissolution, longevity/latitude, and point of initiation having an impact on the effectiveness of the implementation structure; and
- To determine if comprehensiveness is the result of decisive planning or a series of identifiable factors the absence of which renders the current level of problem.

The typical research plan ingredients in the later case would include the following.

Identification of principle actors and administrative responsibility

Determination of the objectives of each operation and the extent of overlap decision making process:

Statistical analysis may be applied to determine the probability of a variety of scenarios, or to determine the descriptive dimensionality of the problem. Scaling and indices development is another tool that may be employed for purpose of sorting out subjective measures of the presence or absence of something deemed potentially problematic. Ranking and relative position measures may be employed to determine patterns of exposure, statistical summaries that allow for a determination of uniqueness versus commonality of exposure, risk, modeling of consequences of the presence of problem, and the implication of the existence of "problem" given a hierarchy of goals and objectives to be achieved with the society.

For those issues declared problematic, i.e., placing the population beyond the level of acceptability with regard to a series of related indicators, explanation is in order. There is a need to identify the cause of the problem. Causal inference is used to explore alternative explanation. The explanations may be found tested within literature if the problem reoccurs or gradually emerges over time. Otherwise, there will be a required period of exploration to find out what is causing the existence of the "problem." If the problem is reoccurring and was deemed severe enough to policy action, the impact of the previous initiatives must be reviewed. There must be a determination as to whether the initiative was effective; whether the degree of increase in severity or dimensionality of the problem exceeded the capacity of the initiative; and, what can be learned from the initiative failure. This means that the sub-objective that were the basis for initiative design must be reviewed and an assessment of the component parts of the initiative conducted to sort out the impact of treatment and other relevant variables. That portion of the outcome that is not explained by the presence of the previous initiative and other specified variables must be reviewed to determine whether there were any operational errors or misspecification of variables.

Review what is known about the relation between variables and the existence of the problem, potential scenarios and the development of forecasts should take place to determine policy options. This requires modeling of relations, decision framing, and usually the use of judgmental methods. With this activity, alternative strategies for addressing the problem are weighted. Multiple criteria approaches to assessing the relative utility of approaches may be explored. Decision mathematics is used to determine likelihood of success. Systems analysis is employed to map out the likely interactive consequences of processes that would be employed with alternatives. Sensitivity analysis may be used to fine tune and simulate the consequences of policy action. And, ultimately, the initiative must be assessed on the basis of likely success versus cost that is normally associated with project evaluation. As a result of the above, recommendations are then made. These recommendations are filtered through a process that compares the potential impact of recommended intervention to the severity of the problem with the goal of avoiding overkill – the use of a bulldozer to move a two ounce rock.

Accepted recommendation requires implementation. The initial execution of policy should have evaluation both formative and summative embedded within it. Formative evaluation is process evaluation. It is the evaluation of everyday operations of the entity that is executing the policy. Summative evaluation is impact evaluation. The assessment of the consequence of policy activity on the stated problem is determination of the achievement of a mandated goal for which the program was designed. Evaluability assessment, that is, the determination of whether the program has been sufficiently executed to be evaluation is conducted at this time. Monitoring strategies for the operations should be defined. And, standards for quality control of operation put into place. The summative evaluation takes place after the program has been completed to determine its relative impact. And, if the problem persists, it may be placed upon the agenda with the review of social conditions beginning again.

A common problem is the temptation of suggesting that one is going to cover everything in a policy issue area. This comes from a term paper mindset that is intellectually comfortable but does not necessarily lead to directed (substantial) attention to the pivotal elements that are key pillars to the opposition's argument.

The topic of specialization should become more refined.

FIGURE 8.2

CONTRASTING ANALOGISTIC FRAMES OF REFERENCE

Immigration and Economic Policy

ORGANISMIC AREA:

Immigration Policy

MECHANISTIC AREA:

Economic Policy

DOMINANT CONCERN:

Violation of Territorial Sovereignty

DOMINANT CONCERN:

Participation in the World Market

UNACCEPTABLE PROBLEM:

Blurred Borders

UNACCEPTABLE PROBLEM:

Enforced Borders

The implications for current and future policy options remains restricted to the frames of reference in which the societal issues are cast. Such restrictiveness might well account for the absence of an immigration component in the various free trade agreements. The perspectives of these two areas could not coexist in the discussion because accompanying the analogy is the rhetoric and restrictive terminology.

The Importance of Conversational Mathematics in the Area of Public Policy

There are a number of areas of further inquiry. The areas listed below serve to further understanding of quantitative techniques that may be applied to emerging Public Policy issues that face us here in the United States and around the world.

Quantitative methods for decision making

Decision Theory

Quasi-experimentation in quantitative policy modeling

Risk Sciences

Calculus for Public Policy

Benefit-Cost analysis and related measures

Meta analysis

Measuring crisis response to natural and unnatural disasters

Regional policy

Intro to management sciences applied to the public sector

Planning and policy making for development

Economic and demographic spatial analysis

Applied research topics for global policy studies

Transnational crime and international security

International aspects of e-governance

Globalization in non-governmental organizations

NGO's development in civil society

Implementation of regional policy

Comparative local governance

World food economy

Multi-national technology and trade

Competing in a global economy

Conflict resolution

The Need for Policy Narratives

Policy narratives, or verbal depictions of reality, are presented as an explanation of societal condition. You see, one of our goals is the evaluation of public policy initiative and it entails a process that replicates the thinking traditionally associated with policy analysis. In the true context of public policy making, both public policy analysis and its subset the evaluation of policy involve the identification of declared societal goals. It's a kind of social eye or identification of discrepancy between what we say our society represents and the aims that we have as a society versus where we actually are. The policy analyst decides whether the discrepancy is problematic through the development and use of mathematical thresholds, the notions of tolerance and severity of condition, based upon an analysis of the stakeholders and any reference input into this problem and the problems are examined for cause. The policy analyst seeks agreement upon indicators of revealed presence of both problem and cause and with the development of those indicators, the analyst is able to develop a design of policy strategies based on theory or explanation pertaining to the cause of the problem. Development and review of indicators, many of which are statistical, or at a minimum, mathematical in their generic form, a review of those indicators of policy execution is essential to assure execution of a plan, and then we develop monitoring points, and those monitoring points are specified for operation phases and stages of the policy that's being executed. Development and execution of corrective action shores up deficiency in planned operation and upon completion the initiatives are addressed for their overall impact so the policy analyst identifies indicators of the summit of impact, of overall operations on the presence of the problem that we've identified, and in addition, the policy analyst identifies indicators of the impact of the overall operation of the presence of the problem within the organizational context of all other entities and initiatives that are designed to address aspects of the same problem. So we have a big job with the major features at each stage involving the measurement of discrepancy and accountability and change.

Discrepancy, accountability, and change become major aspects of what we do in terms of measurement of impact of the recommendations that are presented for public policy discussion and also for an assessment of current societal conditions. You might ask, "Well, how do we think about the specific public policy areas that we are considering in mathematical terms?" I'd like to suggest to you that mathematics itself is used as a way of defining conditions. There's a definitiveness associated with quantification, and the quantification comes after there is an established qualification, and by qualification I'm suggesting that there be a definition of what it is that's being explained. The definition, resting upon the nominal characteristics or qualities of a particular problem and elements of its solution and then we are to ask ourselves how we would measure evidence of the presence or absence of those qualities, and that is where the quantitative element is introduced.

Quality Control

Especially pertinent with regard to environmental policy and all the elements associated with that, in terms of the nature of the components that are released into the air, one can imagine that it would have a special relevance to those individuals who are monitoring the quality of air and water in lieu of potential threats through bio-terror activity.

Quality control can be reduced to statistical equations that you've all ready been exposed to through the use of the t and z tests, at a minimum. But you need to also recognize that there is a whole field of applied mathematics that is directed towards quality control listed as quality control techniques.

Drawing conclusions from limited information

This falls statistically within the realm of probability sampling or sampling techniques that are most usually employed when you're trying to gather information that is too time consuming or overwhelming to attempt to identify all of something, and so there are strategies for the gathering of that information and the assessment of the degree to which the information which has been gathered is truly reflective of the universe of options that are available.

Determining the correctness of conclusion

How likely is it that the conclusion that the policy analyst has arrived at is correct? That discussion is initiated within the area of introductory statistical techniques with the discussion of confidence limits and critical zones. But, understand that there is a whole field of analysis that is referred to as meta-analysis that allows for approaches to looking at a number of studies related to specific kinds of variables and then gleaning what the typical answer has been from a probability standpoint about the nature of the truthfulness of the use of certain variables and the resulting conclusions. Meta-analysis is a review of studies.

Scenarios of uncertainty and scenarios based upon past performance

Scenarios of uncertainty are based upon probability. Risk analysis and risk assessment are the specialized fields of study in the quantitative realm that have to do with these scenarios. There are public policy techniques devoted to the development of alternative scenarios and simulation activities. Scenarios of uncertainty, based upon the likeliness of an occurrence, in a single event or combination of events: Event A having an impact on something that causes Event B, and C and D. The rippling effect, those kinds of possibilities can be stated mathematically and then measured to determine the degree to which the model that has been developed is actually explanatory or truly depictive of the nature of the relationship between variables.

Identifying trends

Trends, translated into the quantitative arena, would be the use of regression equations, either simple or multiple. There is a whole area of mathematical statistics referred to as econometrics that is devoted to, in a more sophisticated fashion, the measurement of change over time. Rate of change, rate of fluctuation, from time period to time period, and the isolation of what is referred to as noise in the calculation of the lines that is depictive of change over time. Those lines may be linear depictions or they may be curved linear, meaning a kind of wave fluctuation.

Comparing groups

It may be groups of individuals. It may be aggregated notions like comparison between two nations or comparison between two economic structures or two approaches to regional development. Those comparisons can be mathematically addressed in a very elementary form through the use of z and t, and then beyond in sophistication given the specific nature of the question to be addressed.

Determining how cases relate to each other

Other statements that may be familiar, that can be bridged into the mathematical realm, like determining how cases relate to each other, which might, in its simplest form, be an issue of identification of relative position of individuals, and perhaps in a much more sophisticated form, the degree of change associated with certain groups or entities that can be compared on the basis of two or more other descriptive traits characteristic of those groups. Most people don't think of correlation analysis in terms of descriptive techniques, but indeed correlation analysis is a descriptive technique and not a predictive technique. For the benefit of those who are less familiar with the mathematical underpinnings of basic statistics, correlation analysis normally appears and is introduced alongside regression analysis under the heading of subdivision of inferential statistics, but in its basic format, correlation analysis is a descriptive array of shift of association between two or more variables for a collection of different groups or individuals.

Determining under what conditions, if any, there are significant differences between cases; determining the potential consequences for cases if certain actions are taken; determining the likely consequences for cases if specific variables are modified. In their simplest form, you can look at these issues in terms of regression-based methodologies (the use of discriminant analysis, analysis of variance, analysis of co-variance, multiple analysis of co-variance.) In a more sophisticated realm, one can look at these kinds of issues in terms of logistical regression, log-linear regression, hazard analysis and other forms of the assessment of the odds of survivability given a shift of conditions. The logic or thought processes behind the use of these elements of conversational mathematics tend to fall within the realm of simulation and development of simulation exercises. One should first identify *Providential* opportunities available for the exercise biblically-informed statesmanship and then prayerfully formulate the pertinent research question.

Having compared the threshold standard to current conditions, the next step is problem declaration. The notion of problem can be very illusive in public policy terms. Problems may be seen as quite severe to some while being perceived as a mere nuisance to others. For this reason, there are approaches to problem formulation, structuring systems that provide greater scrutiny of the decision making process. Statistical analysis can help determine the probability of a variety of scenarios, or to determine the descriptive dimensionality of the "problem." Scaling and index development can serve as tools for sorting out subjective measures of the presence or absence of something deemed potentially problematic. Ranking and relative position measures may be employed to determine patterns of exposure, statistical summaries that allow for a determination of uniqueness versus commonality of exposure, risk, modeling of consequences of the presence of problem, and the implication of the existence of "problem" given a hierarchy of goals and objectives to be achieved within the society.

Coinciding with these milestone activities in the public policy process, are methods and argument structures that allow us to challenge choice of actions.

----What are the underlying assumptions of current policy?

----What is the rationale given for acceptance?

----What are the elements or current policies that are directly linked to the assumptions?

ACTION POINT

Prayerfully return to published works related to your research interest afresh. Explore those documents by using the guidelines below. For each document you review, pinpoint the word picture being presented and critically assess the works given all that has been discussed in this book so far. Remember, the steps you were to take when you began this exploration into biblical statesmanship. Develop your assessment by addressing the following:

1. Statement of what has come before.

2. Schools of thought or points of agreement and disagreement between researchers most cited in the field with regard to the question you are investigating - Recite the genealogy of thought, the progression of key concepts to date and then list the derivatives that have emerged as a consequence of those patterns of thought.

3. Specific pillars of the arguments associated with those dominant perspectives

4. Then, find one case* per school of thought (the assumption here being that there may be competing schools of thought each of which resting on premises that are antithetical to biblical understanding. Choose – just one case that reflects common place occurrence so that critics will not be able to dismiss your case as an aberration. Make sure the case you explore meets the definitional context(s) requirements of the researchers that have gone before, and proceed to describe in great detail all of the salient attributes that should be a natural outgrowth of the case if indeed the underlying assumptions being made by the prominent researchers is true. I suggest that you tackle no more than three schools of thought at a time. If there are more, make sure you address the two most prominent, ones that represent collectively approximately 90 percent of the publications as the foundational orientation of the published studies. Again, by case, I am referring to a context, location, or situation that meets the terms associated with the competing school of thought in your research area. The logic is this. Credibility of explanation rests on whether or not evidence exists pointing to an outcome that differs from what would be expected if the prevailing theory (explanation) were true.

5. Prayerfully identify the scriptural address of the topic you are investigating and then proceed to assess each case on the basis of the biblical principles being overlooked in the case that would otherwise have been handled differently if conventional "wisdom" were applied: starting with how the problem is defined and then progressing to the point at which terms would be defined and measured.

Because you will have outlined the themes and propositions that are commonly understood by prominent researchers, you should go to your case and start your checklist with seeing if those things be present or absent. Then, proceed to delineate those attributes that are present that fail to be accounted for by current researchers. Once you have completed this exercise, write a summation. And, then write a paragraph of conclusions, closing with the implications and what that should mean for the direction of future research or public sector action.

Do not despise small beginnings as the above steps may open up public sector discourse to consideration of a God-Honoring approach to your topic of inquiry.

CONCLUSION

Acknowledging God in the Exercise of Biblical Statesmanship

"Don't be overcome by evil, but overcome evil with good!"[112]
Romans 12:21, New American Standard Bible

The admonition of Romans 12:21 should drive the exercise of biblical statesmanship. Likewise, the use of words, the power of definition, should be appreciated in all of its potency to either bless our curse the workings of governance. The outcome of that use of words will depend on the heart of that Ambassador of Christ, equipped with biblical understanding, who prayerfully answers the God-given calling to respond to the needs of the nation, a response that has significance even for other nations. The notion of the world as occupied territory with followers of Christ operating behind enemy lines as C.S. Lewis puts it is an intriguing notion. That idea suggests that this present life is a place where true followers are not to become too comfortable. To not conform to this world's system of operation, but to be transformed by the renewing of our minds is expected of us by the Commander of Hosts.

Part of conforming to this world at the level of nation would entail alignment with the enemies of Israel. Such an alignment is not an acceptable posture in the eyes of God, yet remains entertained by many who claim to be *Christ's followers*.

Many fail to recognize the connection between right acknowledgment of God and the quality of life the population experiences under the authority of its leadership. This book attempted initiate the discussion of governance mechanisms that break down when right relationship with God is absent. Failure to acknowledge God's rule has adverse consequences. Both believer and unbeliever are invited to see for themselves the results of acknowledging God in the decisions of state. Willard makes this point.

> God as personality is not a physical reality that everyone must see whether they want to or not. He can, of course, make himself present to the human mind in any way he chooses. But, for good reasons rooted deeply in the nature of the person and of personal relationships-his preferred way is to speak, to communicate: thus the absolute centrality of scripture to our discipleship. And this, among other things, is the reason why an extensive use of solitude and silence is so basic for growth of the human spirit for they form an appropriate context for listening and speaking to God.[113]

Given this reality, the acknowledgment of God is not simply a ceremonial act but a real transformation on the heart and mind of the individual so that in right relationship with Christ, the mind is transformed and sanity is restored. As a consequence, a disciple is someone who is learning from Jesus how to live this life.

Moving Toward Biblical Statesmanship

A common assumption is that public policy analysis among secularists is that discourse should be *value-neutral* (their notion of empirical) when it comes to issues of "faith" in a one-size fits-all world, avoiding the endorsement of any one particular worldview. This assumption is false in the sense that methods texts that state no particular philosophical view are indeed most frequently communicating a secular worldview. Sometimes authors communicate a religious worldview, perhaps without actually recognizing it. For example, the title, "Eight-Fold Path," is associated with Eastern religious belief.[114] Moreover, New Age thinking has heavily entrenched the nature of public policy conversations, if not directly, then indirectly in the way public policy problems are couched, the terminology employed, and the priorities. So, this book which is speaks unapologetically about decision-making that has as it point of departure the belief that Christ rules. May the Lord Jesus Christ receive the glory.

Pitfalls experienced in theory or explanation construction that lead to poor policy would include the problem of fallacy and related maladies in the use of rhetoric through which the basic policy questions become cast. Perhaps an even more critical dilemma is that posed by the prevalence of confusing description with explanation. Description is defined by Webster as, "the act of describing; specifically, the discourse intended to give a mental image of something to discuss 'what' contributed to the existence of that thing. *"[115] We appear to be trapped by demographic imagery that allows us to describe the characteristics of those that are experiencing a social problem but not present is the analysis that leads to a policy action based upon causality.*

As biblically informed decision makers, we must develop God-honoring policy narratives. Policy narratives, or verbal depictions of reality, carry explanations for societal condition.

As a biblically informed decision-maker, you should describe in writing what God would say about what you see.

This requires a depth of prayerful analysis that goes beyond singling out of context an isolated bible verse. You must allow God to renew your mind by giving you insights in the Holy Bible. For each passage of Holy Scripture, concentrate by asking questions all that transpires in the passage and the details concerning the actions that are taking place. We interpret Holy Scripture with Holy Scripture and ask God to reveal to the meaning and relevance for the issue at hand. Explore what should be known about God's view that we may gain from the passage in order to grow in the Power of the Holy Spirit.

Write down the insights you gain through your prayerful search through the Bible. Resolve to inquire of the Lord devoting your thoughts, and writing to His service along with all your other actions. Pray that the Lord grant you His guidance through His Holy Spirit and in the obedience to His written Word, the Holy Bible. Prerequisite, of course, is saving knowledge of our Lord and Savior Jesus Christ. It is in right relationship with Christ Jesus that He is made unto us Wisdom.

As a biblically informed decision maker, compare what you see with what the secularist sees. Write a description of what the world sees in response to the following questions.

- How might assumptions translate into policy? In other words, what would policy look like if we were to apply assumptions that the world deems "appropriate."
- What are the chances of acceptance of these assumptions?
- Can we overcome those obstacles? If so, how should the obstacles be overcome and in what timeframe?

- What are the most appropriate criteria for assessing future policy initiatives?
- What outcome(s) should be avoided at all cost?
- If tradeoffs exist, what is expendable in what situations?
- Who should be held accountable for what?

The sovereignty of the United States and the well-being of the rest of the nations of the world are jeopardized when our leaders fail to acknowledge God in the decisions of state. That is because our democratic political structure of governance assumes moral character, traits supportive of God's idea of "good" then shared among government decision-makers.

Given the number of climatic challenges present in recent times, the question of God looms large. C.S. Lewis, a noted scholar and excellent storyteller, somewhere once posed this interesting scenario---that of God being outside the confines of time---peering in through the window in an effort not only to see but also to get the attention of humanity. Picking up the world and holding it as if holding a small box that has people in it, God turns the box. He tilts the box. He shakes the box--- all in the effort to get the attention of those inside. I thought of this word picture as I heard the latest news of yet one more natural disaster.

Natural disasters are increasing in both frequency and severity. They are worsening the conditions of underdeveloped regions where social plight abounds. The aftermath of natural disasters bears both external political and national security implications. Such devastated places become the breeding ground for transnational criminal activity and provide safe harbor for enemies of the United States. Meanwhile, here in the United States, we forget that we too are susceptible to such forms of natural calamity including the dreaded tsunami. Indeed, researchers have found that the combination of population density, natural wealth density, and aging infrastructure coupled with natural calamity yield much greater loss.

Is Humanity Willing to Hear this Message? Perhaps, Not Yet!

While a scholarly conference on Religion and Politics was going on a few years ago in Virginia Beach, celebrating the strong Judeo-Christian roots to our nation's founding, something else eventful was occurring just an hour away in the fair city of Williamsburg, Virginia.

During the 400th anniversary of the region commemorating the dedication of the United States to the God of the Holy Bible, Williamsburg served as the site for the Winter Democratic National Committee Meeting. President Bush was in attendance, exhibiting a willingness to work together with the Democratic Party in the governance of our country. It is important to note that at that same Democrat sponsored Williamsburg meeting, Al-Husainy, an anti-Semitic Imam of Dearborn Michigan, prayed the opening prayer of the event. His prayer which may be viewed online at Hotair was as follows:

> "We thank you god, to bless us among your creations. We thank you, god, to make us a great nation. We thank you, god to send us your messages through our father Abraham, and Jesus and Mohammed, through you, god, we unite, so guide us to the right spot we wish for peace, equality and help us to stop the war and violence, and **oppression and occupation**." [February 2, 2007][116]

Al-Husainy, the person that the political party decided to have lead prayer at their meeting, leads one of the largest Shi'ite Mosques in the United States.

There is an abysmal tenor to recanting this story, a story of multicultural absurdity that would have been seen as an intolerable affront to our nation at war time even just a decade ago. At least two things are troubling here. One being the political party's desensitized choice of prayer warrior; and, the second, being the message that such a choice for invocation makes. The choice of Al-Husainy as prayer warrior shouts to those engaged in the war effort, "Extremely Weak Resolve here!" It heralds a "Don't count on us"- philosophy on the part of a major political party. By the choice of Al-Husainy to lead prayer, Party faithful were also saying in clear terms, "We will neither tangibly nor even symbolically stand by or for Israel."

As far as the message goes, Al-Husainy's prayer concludes with the words "*oppression*" and "*occupation.*" These word choices are not harmless. They tell a sinister tale, too! With Al-Husainy chosen as the spiritual voice box of the political party event, theatrically scripted and received by D.N.C. faithful, Al-Husainy paints unapologetically yet again a word picture of the United States and Israel as Satan---a depiction given to our nation by our enemies, foreign and more apparently now, domestic. Take note: Al-Husainy called our nation names and there has not even been a whimper of outrage on the part of any major Party notable as a consequence to date.

God says in the Holy Bible that we are to have no other gods before Him.

For those who believe in the ***inerrancy of the Holy Bible*** the fact is that our unchangeable God did indeed make the following statement found in Genesis 12:3 regarding Israel,

"And I will bless them that bless thee and curse him that curseth thee; and in thee shall all nations of the earth be blessed."

***

GOD'S view of all of the nations of the world is expressed in Psalm 2 of the Holy Bible:

"Why do the nations assemble with commotion [uproar and confusion of voices], and why do the people imagine (meditate upon and devise) an empty scheme?

The kings of the earth take their places the rulers take counsel together against the Lord and His Anointed One (the Messiah, the Christ). They say, [Acts 4:25-27]

Let us break Their bands [of restraint] asunder and cast Their cords [of control] from us.

He Who sits in the heavens laughs; the Lord has them in derision [and in supreme contempt He mocks them].

He speaks to them in His deep anger and troubles (terrifies and confounds) them in His displeasure and fury, saying,

Yet have I anointed (installed and placed) My King [firmly] on My holy hill of Zion.

I will declare the decree of the Lord: He said to Me, You are My Son; this day [I declare] I have begotten You. [Heb. 1:5; 3:5, 6; II Pet. 1:17,18.]

Ask of Me, and I will give You the nations as Your inheritance, and the uttermost parts of the earth as Your possession.

You shall dash them in pieces like potters' ware. [Rev. 12:5; 19:15]

Now therefore, O you kings, act wisely; be instructed and warned, O you rulers of the earth.

Serve the Lord with reverent awe and worshipful fear; rejoice and be in high spirits with trembling [lest you displease Him].

Kiss the Son [pay homage to Him in purity], lest He be angry and you perish in the way, for soon shall His wrath be kindled. O blessed (happy, fortunate, and to be envied) are all those who seek refuge and put their trust in Him!" Psalm 2, the Holy Bible, Amplified Version

ACTION POINT

OFFER REAL HOPE BY PRAYERFULLY CONSULTING GOD

I said, "O Sovereign Lord, you alone know."[117]

One must diligently study the Bible daily. **"All Scripture is inspired by God and profitable for teaching, for reproof, for correction, for training in righteousness; that the man of God may be adequate, equipped for every good work." (II Tim 3:16-17)** Pray before you read the Holy Bible. Keep short accounts with God. Confession and true repentance is required to eliminate distance that comes from being in sin. Acknowledge the salvation that Jesus has offered as you ask the Holy Spirit to guide your prayers. Pray that the Holy Spirit might draw you ever closer to the Father through Jesus Christ so that you may grow in the understanding of His precepts and ways.

The biblically sound interface with government is that of *Godly statesmanship—God-fearing statesmanship values what God values* and pursues those things under the direction of the Holy Spirit as confirmed in the *Holy Bible.* All ideas must be tested on the basis of Holy Scripture. Then, it is time to develop biblically informed narratives.

With all the above, it is critical to remember that the most important analytical tool at your disposal is the Holy Bible. The Bible is indeed for *"the government of the people, by the people, for the people."* Test all policy options, innovative ideas, and alliances on the Holy Bible. As one grows in spiritual maturity through the power and presence of the Holy Spirit in right acknowledgment of God, God, Himself, will make our path straight.

GOD Speed!

SUGGESTED BIBLICAL CHARACTER STUDY EXAMPLES TO EXPLORE

Examples of public works management: Nehemiah, David

Examples of the role of clergy: Ezra, Nathan

Example of biblical statesmanship: Daniel, Joseph, Deborah, Esther

STEWARDSHIP EXAMPLES

Examples of crying out to the Lord: Moses, Paul, Mary, the Early Church

Examples of prosperity: Solomon, Hezekiah, Jehosaphat, the Early Church

CHARACTER PITFALLS TO AVOID

Examples of self absorption: Cain, Balaam, Asa, Prodigal son, Judas, Peter in Denial

Examples of idolatry: rich young ruler (who later became Barnabas, it is alleged), period of the deluge, and Sodom/Gomorrah

Examples of distance from God: Adam, Balaam, Peter

Examples of depression: Naomi, Saul, David, Elijah, Jonah, Ahab

Examples of lethargy: Jonah, Ahab, Elijah

Examples of futility: Ahab, Asa, Nahman

NOTES FOR PREFACE

[1] See Prologue to the Holy Bible translation of 1384 by John Wycliffe

[2] C.S. Lewis, *Mere Christianity*, New York, NY: Harper Collins, 2001, p. 80.

[3] Comment made Rev Lee Earl of Shiloh Baptist Church, Alexandria Virginia during his Wilberforce Symposium Address.

[4] This accusation has been raised by such as Madeleine Albright, *The Mighty and the Almighty: Reflections on America, God, and World Affairs*, New York: HarperCollins, Publishers, 2006; and, others have simply criticized the language employed by religious movements. See Charles Kimball, *When Religion Becomes Evil*, San Francisco: HarperCollins, 2002.

[5] Galatians 5:22-23, *Holy Bible*

[6] See Acts, Chapter 17. *Holy Bible*

[7] See Genesis, Chapter 11: 1-9, *Holy Bible*

[8] *Middle East Media Research Institute (MEMRI), the August 9, 2003, edition of the Egyptian weekly al-Ahram al-Arabi.*

NOTES FOR CHAPTER 1

[9] *Romans 1: 21-23, Holy Bible*, New International Version

[10] Stephen McDowell and Mark Beliles, *Liberating the Nations: Biblical Principles of Government, Education, Economics, & Politics.* (Charlottesville, VA: The Providence Foundation, 1995)123. For related discussions see, Gary T. Amos, *Defending the Declaration: How the Bible and Christianity Influenced the Writing of the Declaration of Independence*, (Charlottesville, VA: The Providence Foundation, 1989); Mark A. Beliles and Douglas S. Anderson, *Contending for the Constitution: Recalling the Christian Influence on the Writing of the Constitution and the Biblical Basis of American Law and Liberty*, (Charlottesville, VA: The Providence Foundation, 2005); Stephen K. McDowell, Building Godly Nations: Lessons from the Bible and America's Christian History, (Charlottesville, VA: The Providence Foundation, 2004).

[11] Stephen L. Carter, *God's Name in Vain: The Wrongs and Rights of Religion in Politics*. (New York: Basic Books, 2000)

[12] Rogers M. Smith, *Civic Ideals* (New Haven: Yale University Press, 1997) 1

[13] *Ibid.*

[14] Stephen L. Carter, *God's Name in Vain: The Wrongs and Rights of Religion in Politics*. (New York: Basic Books, 2000)

[15] Stephen L. Carter, *God's Name in Vain*, 83

[16] *Ibid.*

[17] *Ibid.*

[18] Carter, *God's Name in Vain*, 93

[19] Harris, Sam. *The End of Faith: Religion, Terror, and the Future of Reason*, (New York: W.W. Norton & Company, 2005) 103

[20] Harris, *The End of Faith*, 103

[21] Harris, *The End of Faith*, 106

[22] Recommended reading on transformation within ourselves may be found in the work of Larry Crabb entitled, Inside *Out: Real Change Is Possible --If You're Willing to Start from the Inside Out* (Colorado Springs, Colorado: Navpress 1988). In no way is there justification for ignoring the public square, a point that can readily be seen in the work of Francis J. Beckwith, *Politics for Christians: Statecraft as Soulcraft, (Downers Grove, Illinois: Intervarsity Press, 2010)*. Do understand that the condition of one's relationship with God must have primacy over any other endeavor, if one's steps are to be ordered by Him. See Proverbs 3: 5-7, Holy Bible, which offers the scriptural basis for the book you are now reading, Acknowledging God in the Decisions of State.

[23] Genesis 4: 1-17, *Holy Bible, King James Version.*

[24] Dallas Willard, *The Divine Conspiracy: Rediscovering Our Hidden Life in God*. (San Francisco: Harper, 1998)177. Also, see the following references for an explanation of the link between relationship with God and prevailing thought. For a discussion of personal relationship with God, see Dallas Willard. *Hearing God: Developing Conversational Relationship with God, (*Downers Grove, IL: InterVarsity Press, 1999). The implications for science may be found in Gerald L. Schroeder *The Science of God: The Convergence of Scientific and Biblical Wisdom*, (New York: The Free Press, 1997). .Malcolm A.Jeeves and R. J. Barry in *Science, Life, and Christian Belief: A Survey of Contemporary Issues,* (Grand Rapids, MI: Bakers Books,

1998). R.C. Sproul *The Consequences of Ideas: Understanding the Concepts that Shaped Our World. (*Wheaton, IL: Crossway Books, 2000). And, see Edward T. Welch. *When People are Big and God is Small: Overcoming Peer Pressure, Codependency, and the Fear of Man.* (Phillipsburg, NJ: P& R Publishing, 1997). A warning is given in David Jeremiah. *Invasion of Other Gods: The Seduction of New Age Spirituality,* (Dallas: Word Publishing, 1995). [24] *Lewis, Op Cit.*, p.85
1: 21-23, Holy Bible.
[25] *Lewis, Op Cit.*, p.85
[26] Romans 1:18-25, *Holy Bible, New International Version*
[27] Leviticus 26:14-18, *Holy Bible, Amplified Version*
[28] Donald G. Bloesch *Faith and Its Counterfeits*, (Downers Grove, Ill: InterVarsity Press, 1981) 77.
[29] Oswald Chambers, *My Utmost for His Highest.* (Grand Rapids, Michigan: Discovery House, 1992).
[30] Rabbi Abraham J. Twerski, *Living Each Day.* Brooklyn, (New York: Mesorah Publications, Ltd., 2001)361. Also See, Isaiah 51:1-2, the Holy Bible.
[31] 1 Kings 18:21, *Holy Bible, Livvy Translation*
[32] See the writings of Jonathan Edwards to understand the moral underpinnings that come with Christian revival.
Visit:http://onlinebooks.library.upenn.edu/webbin/book/lookupname?key=Edwards%2C%20Jonathan%2C%201703-1758
[33] Bloesch, *Op Cit.*,77. Also See, 1Kings 18:21, *Holy Bible*, New International Version

NOTES FOR CHAPTER 2

[34] *Romans 1: 21-23, Holy Bible.*

[35] The question might be asked, "What is wrong with continuing with the eclectic mindset?" The answers come in reviewing a number of works that point to the relation between mental focus and quality of life, both physical and spiritual. See the following works: James Allen. *As A Man Thinketh.* New York: Barnes & Noble Books, 1992; Donald Grey Barnhouse. *Romans,* Grand Rapids, MI: Wm. B. Eerdmans Publishing Company, 1999; Harry Blamires. *The Christian Mind: How Should a Christian Think?* Grand Rapids, MI: Family Christian Press, 1963; Larry Crabb. *Inside Out.* Colorado Springs, CO: Navpress, 1988; Emil Brunner. *Christianity and Civilization: Specific Problems.* New York: Charles Scribner's Sons, 1949; Victoria Lee Erickson and Michelle Lim Jones(eds.) *Surviving Terror: Hope and Justice in a World of Violence.* Grand Rapids, MI: Brazos Press, 2002; Richard J. Foster, *Celebration of Discipline: The Path to Spiritual Growth.* New York: HarperCollins Publication, 1988; Gary A Haugen. *Good News about Injustice.* Downers Grove, IL: InterVarsity Press, 1999; C.S. Lewis, *Mere Christianity.* New York: Simon & Schuster, 1980; Tremper Longman. *Reading the Bible with Heart and Mind,* Colorado Springs, CO.: Navpress, 1997; Franky Schaeffer. *Addicted to Mediocrity: 20th Century Christians and the Arts.* Wheaton, IL: Crossway Books, 1981; R.C. Sproul, *Renewing Your Mind: Basic Christian Beliefs You Need to Know.* Grand Rapids, MI: Baker Book, 1998.; Ron Tagliapietra,. *Better Thinking and Reasoning.* Greenville, SC: Bob Jones University Press, 1995; R.A. Torrey, *What the Bible Teaches.* New Kensington, PA: Whitaker House, 1996; Turner, Mark. *Cognitive Dimensions of Social Science: The Way We Think About Politics, Economics, Law, and*

Society. New York: Oxford University Press, 2001; and, Isaac Watts, *Improvement of the Mind: A Supplement to Logic,* Morgan, PA: Soli Deo Gloria Publications, 1998.

[36] Psalm 107: 13, *Holy Bible*

[37] *Source: http://www.annefrank.com/2_life_excerpts.htm*

[38] C.S. Lewis, *Mere Christianity, p. 106*

[39] Leviticus 26, *Holy Bible*

[40] A.W. Tozer, *The Knowledge of the Holy.* (New York: HarperCollins Publishers, 1961)103

[41] *Ibid.*

[42] *Ibid.*

[43] Brian Hogwood and Lewis A. Gunn, *Public Policy in the Real World (New York: Oxford University Press, 1984)*

[44] William N. Dunn *Public Policy Analysis: An Introduction.*2nd. Edition (Upper Saddle River, NJ: Prentice Hall, 1994)

[45] See Stephen L. Carter, *God's Name in Vain: the Wrongs and Rights of Religion in Politics.* (New York: Basic Books, 2000).

According to Carter, the reasoning was this *Lord's gently pro-slavery pamphlet is less important for his argument than for his style of argument. Once having argued, in a reflective and scholarly way, that Slavery was consistent with the will of God,he concluded firmly, "That all contrary suppositions, theories, and interpretations must be false, wherever the fallacy lies. The source of the fallacy was, for Lord, "specious humanitarian philosophy," which "substitutes the natural sentiments, sympathies, tastes, volitions, purposes, and resolves of the human mind for supernatural grace; or puts the latter in subserviency to the former. According to Carter, "Here Lord was making a rhetorical move that truly believing religionists, sooner Or later, have no choice but to make. If God wills a **proposition P,** God cannot also **Will Not P;** so those who believe that God's will is actually Not P are in error. Lord took the View, in other words, that God could not simultaneously be for slavery and against it; that is, God could not hold to **P** and **Not P** at the same time. The reason is that God, being Perfect, cannot be the author of any contradiction. This is a very old proposition in theology, going back to Thomas Aquinas and, before him, to Aristotle. Thus the Pro-slavery preachers and the anti-slavery preachers agreed on at least one premise: A Perfect God could not be on both sides of the issue simultaneously. The preachers of the Second Great Awakening believed in doing God's work in the world. If God's will was **P** rather than **Not P,** then **P** rather and **Not P** was what the world should reflect. And if the world instead continued to reflect **Not P,** it was the duty of God's people to change it, until **P** was both God's Word and living truth. If God's immutable Word, **P,** condemned slavery as a sin, then God's creation had to be made free of the practice. Nowadays, as we have seen, a significant body of thought holds that activism of this kind is a bad idea, perhaps prohibited by the Constitution. It will be instructive, therefore, to consider who Americans caught up in the debate over slavery in the first half of the nineteenth century conceptualized what might now be described as a conflict between church and state.*

[46] See Gordon Mursell, editor, The Story of Christian Spirituality: Two Thousand Years, from East to West (Minneapolis: Fortress Press, 2001) 329.

[47] Harris, Sam. *The End of Faith: Religion, Terror, and the Future of Reason* (New York: W.W. Norton & Company, 2005) 103

[48] Carter, *God's Name in Vain,* 85 - Carter goes on to say, Parker, Finney, and others preached against slavery during the first half of the Nineteenth century, the years leading up to the Civil

War. *"This was an era in which, we might say, the question of the proper role of public religious argument in the nation's affairs was very much in play. In one of the peculiarly American historical paradoxes, fears that the country's religious affairs might come to be dominated by institutional religions were leading, not to a high wall of separation between church and state, but to the burgeoning "Christian nation" sentiment. One reason might have been that the fear about the influence of religion, as many historians have shown, was really a fear about the growing influence of the Roman Catholic Church. Protestants after all understood the Idea of "church" somewhat differently than Catholics did, and could easily envision a nation wholly Christian with its institutional religions wholly disestablished.*

Thus, the abolitionist fervor probably assisted the young nation in working out its views on what weight should be given to claims by religious leaders about what direction God wanted the country to take. Here after all, were clergy---lots and lots of clergy---contending that the nation was obliged, both morally and spiritually, to free the slaves, for no other reason than that slaveholding was inconsistent with Divine Law. What the nation had to decide was not, at first, whether the antislavery preachers were right, but whether to listen at all.

On the other hand, Nathan Lord, the president of Dartmouth College, according to Carter, "argued that all human institutions, including slavery, serve in some mysterious way 'the all-wise purposes of God'." Carter says that Lord warned against "Utopian" thought and the zeal to found the New Jerusalem before its time.

[49] Bernard J. Coughlin. *Church and State in Social Welfare* (New York: Columbia University Press, 1965). Also see Axel R. Schaefer. "Evangelicalism, Social Reform and the US Welfare State, 1970-1996," pp. 249-273, in David K. Adams and Cornelius A. van Minnem, eds., *Religious and Secular Reform in America: Ideas, Beliefs, and Social Change.* New York: New York University Press, 1999).

[50] *Ibid, p. 249*

[51] Coughlin, *Op.Cit.*251-258; also see, Alan Mittleman, Robert Licht, & Jonathan D. Sarna. *Jews and the American Public Square: Debating Religion and Republic (*New York: Rowman & Littlefield, 2002).

[52] Ben Shapiro, "Self-hating Jews and the Jewish State, Town Hall.com, Wednesday, July 26, 2006.

[53] Astri Suhrke, "The Limits of State-building: The Role of International Assistance in Afghanistan." Paper presented at the International Studies Association Annual Meeting, San Diego 21-24, March 2006.

[54] Tet-Lim N. Yee, Jews, Gentiles and Ethnic Reconciliation: Paul's Jewish Identity and Ephesians, (New York: Cambridge University Press, 2005).

[55] Sheri Ross Gordon, "Inside Jews for Jesus" *Reform Judaism,* 22 (Winter 1993), 22-27,

[56] Stephen Zunes,"Why the U.S. Supports Israel" Foreign Policy In Focus, *FPIF Policy Report,* May 2002.

[57]Tet-Lim N. Yee, Jews, Gentiles and Ethnic Reconciliation: Paul's Jewish Identity and Ephesians, (New York: Cambridge University Press, 2005).

[58] Ben Shapiro, "Self-hating Jews and the Jewish State, Town Hall.com, Wednesday, July 26, 2006.

[59] John Cloud, August 24, 1998, vol. 152, No. 8, p. 66. Time Magazine,"For They Know Not What They Do." David Barrett, George Kurian and Todd Johnson. *World Christian Encyclopedia*, 2nd Edition, (New York: Oxford University Press, 2001).

[60] Mark Beaird, "Coping with An Angry World" www.markbeaird.org/assets/pdf/prev/coping_with_an **angry_world**.pdf -2006. Also see, Roger Kimball, Tenured Radicals. (Chicago, Il: Ivan R. Dee, Publisher, 1998).

[61] See Erwin W. Lutzer, *Hitler's Cross* (Chicago: Moody Press, 1995). Also see, Paul Johnson, *A History of the Jews* (New York: Harper Row Publishers, 1987). To further understand the dynamics of interaction between ethnic histories and the perception of the church, see Daniel Juster, *The Biblical World View: An Apologetic* (San Francisco: International Scholars Publications, 1995); and, Mark A. Noll, *Turning Points: Decisive Moments in the History of Christianity*. 2d. (Grand Rapids, Michigan: Baker Academic, 2000).

[62] A series of steps remain associated with the logic of written argument. The account given here represents a condensed version of what could be gleaned from any rhetoric text on the mechanics of building an argument. A. M. Tibbetts, *The Strategies of Rhetoric* (Tibbetts 1969) and M. Scriven, *Reasoning* (Scriven 1976) lead my list as being particularly insightful and well-deserving of special mention. Indeed, Tibbetts maintains that the exchange of ideas in the form of argument serve as a foundation for the pursuit of Truth. Both of the above mentioned authors stress understanding the architectural structure of written argument. See A.M. Tibbett *The Strategies of Rhetoric*. Glenview, Ill: Scotts Foresman, 1969;M. Scriven. *Reasoning*. New York: McGraw Hill, 1976; Olivia M. McDonald *Analytical Bridge for the Literary Mind: A Unique Primer for Public Policy Discourse*. A Limited Access Document (c) 2006.

NOTES FOR CHAPTER 3

[63] *Romans 1: 21-23, Holy Bible*, New International Version

[64] Luke 11:23, *Holy Bible*, New International Version

[65] John 15:5, *Holy Bible*, English Standard Version

[66] SOURCE: http://www.dictionary.net/honor

[67] Some have quipped that the American citizens should read the Quran so that they will know what is in it and then in outrage and disgust, act accordingly. My response differs. It would be better if the Church would read the Holy Bible and apply the principles therein so that the light of God's presence in our lives would be so manifestly seen by all that even our enemies-- *any* who may wish to be our fear-generating jailer-- would cry out, "*What must I do to be saved?*"

NOTES FOR CHAPTER 4

[68] *Matthew 12:33, Holy Bible*

[69] Paul Tillich, "Lost Dimension in Religion," *Saturday Evening Post* magazine (1960, Richard Thruelsen and John Kobler, Editors) 51-52

[70] Twerski, Op. Cit., 389

[71]Ezekiel 12:2 and Ezekiel 14:3-5, *Holy Bible*, Amplified Version

[72] Matthew 8:5-13, *Holy Bible,* New Living Version

[73] *See Brian Hogwood and B. Guy Peters, Policy Dynamics (New York: St. Martin Press, 1983)*

[74] Guy Peters, *American Public Policy: Promise and Performance*, 7th Edition, 2006. Also see, B. Guy Peters, K.M. Frans, and Van Nispen. *Public Policy Instruments* (Northampton, MA: Edward Elgar Publishing Limited, 1998)

[75] Prologue to the Bible translation of 1384, by John Wycliffe

[76] See Stephen McDowell and Mark Beliles, *Liberating the Nations: Biblical Principles of Government, Education, Economics, & Politics* (Charlottesville, VA: The Providence Foundation, 1995)123. For related discussions, see, Gary T. Amos, *Defending the Declaration: How the Bible and Christianity Influenced the Writing of the Declaration of Independence*, (Charlottesville, VA: The Providence Foundation, 1989); Mark A. Beliles and Douglas S. Anderson, *Contending for the Constitution: Recalling the Christian Influence on the Writing of the Constitution and the Biblical Basis of American Law and Liberty*, (Charlottesville, VA: The Providence Foundation, 2005); Stephen K. McDowell, *Building Godly Nations: Lessons from the Bible and America's Christian History*, (Charlottesville, VA: The Providence Foundation, 2004).

[77] There are many Bible-Believing Scientists I could point to so that you may know that prayerfully consulting the Holy Bible is not new to the scientific community. However, I have chosen just one. If you wish more examples, I recommend that you read the book entitled, *Biblical Basis for Modern Science*, by Henry M. Morris (Green Forest, AR: Master Books, 2002). For now, I invite you to cons consider **Louis Pasteur**, the father of *"pasteurization,"* in response to his prayerful study of the written Word of God in attempt to discover what was causing the onslaught of disease in a community, had his eyes land on the following verse:"Through faith we understand that the worlds were framed by the word of God, so that things which are seen were not made of things which do appear." Hebrews 11:3 KJV"That which is invisible comes from that which is invisible." Hebrews 11:3 [*My Paraphrase*] Do Note: Pasteur did not use that singular verse as a "tag-along" to his own thin collection of thoughts. No, He started with that verse as the driving force behind his research. Accepting the entire Holy Bible as true, relevant, worth acting on, Pasteur proceeded to devise his research agenda based on Truth. Pasteur decided to dig deeply into the truthfulness of that statement found in the written word of God, the Holy Bible! As an extension of that Biblical understanding, Pasteur decided that it may be necessary to rid impurities from food substances, impurities that are not detectable with the "naked eye." From the reasoning process consistent with the written Word of God and no doubt guided by the Presence of the Holy Spirit, Pasteur arrives at what we now refer to as "Germ" Theory, thus saving millions of lives from that biblically-based insight. He took that Bible Truth and then actively searched out/investigated. His study resulted in fruitfulness. Here is Pasteur's account in his own words: "Blessed is he who carries within himself God and an ideal and who obeys it — an ideal of art, of science, or Gospel virtues. Therein lie the springs of great thoughts and great actions; they all reflect light from the Infinite. (*The Wordsworth Dictionary of Quotations*, 1998 by Connie Robertson, p. 320)

NOTES FOR CHAPTER 5

[78] *Matthew12:30, Holy Bible*

[79] *1Corinthians 1:20, Holy Bible*

[80] See Y. Dror, *Policymaking under Adversity*. (New Brunswick, N.J.: Transaction Books, 1986) Also see, Rhys Edward Dryzek, *Discursive Democracy: Politics, Policy, and Political Science*. (New York: Cambridge University Press, 1990); D. Yankelovich and I.M. Destler (eds) *Beyond the Beltway: Engaging the Public in U.S. Foreign Policy*. (New York: W.W. Norton & Company, 1994). Also see, T. H. Henriksen (ed.) *Foreign Policy for America in the Twenty-First Century: Alternative Perspectives*, (Stanford, CA.: Hoover Institution Press, 2001)

[81] See Y. Dror, *Policymaking under Adversity*. (New Brunswick, N.J.: Transaction Books, 1986) Also see, Rhys Edward Dryzek, *Discursive Democracy: Politics, Policy, and Political Science*. (New York: Cambridge University Press, 1990); D. Yankelovich and I.M. Destler (eds) *Beyond the Beltway: Engaging the Public in U.S. Foreign Policy*. (New York: W.W. Norton & Company, 1994). Also see, T. H. Henriksen (ed.) *Foreign Policy for America in the Twenty-First Century: Alternative Perspectives*, (Stanford, CA.: Hoover Institution Press, 2001)

[82] *A Well-Reasoned Response: A Systematic Theory for the Evaluation of Progress Made by Security and Defense Initiatives in the Western Hemisphere* by Olivia M. McDonald (2010), p. 56-60.

NOTES FOR CHAPTER 6

[83] *Matthew 12:34, Holy Bible, Amplified Version*

[84] Willard, *The Divine Conspiracy*, 277

[85] For a comprehensive view of the secular scholarly literature that pertains to the challenges that I have chosen to approach from a biblical perspective, see *Theories of the Policy Process* by Paul A. Sabatier (Cambridge, MA: Westview Press, 2007)- as found at the link entitled Theories of the Policy Process-Estudios PostGrado at https://cursodeposgrado.files.wordpress.com/2011/08/libro-sabatier.pdf

[86] 2 Timothy 3:16-17, *Holy Bible*

[87] Ezekiel 37:1-3, *Holy Bible*

[88] The following works are recommended: Richard J. Foster, *Celebration of Discipline: The Path to Spiritual Growth*, (New York: HarperCollins, 1998); Richard J. Foster and James Bryan Smith, Devotional Classics: Selected Readings for Individuals and Groups (New York: HarperCollins, 1993)

[89] Stinchcombe, *Op.Cit.*

[90] See Eugene Bardach, *Practical Guide for Policy Analysis: Eightfold Path to More Effective Problem Solving*. (Thousand Oaks, Cage: Sage Publication, 2012).

NOTES FOR CHAPTER 7

[91] *Matthew 12:43-45, Holy Bible, New Living Translation*

[92] See: Lutzer, *Op.Cit.*, 2002; Noll, *Op.Cit.*; and, Thomas Sowell, *Black Rednecks and White Liberals (San Francisco, CA: Encounter Books, 2005)*.

[93] Steven Smith and Michael Sosin, "The Varieties of Faith-Related Agencies" *Public Administration Review* (2001) 61: 651–670. doi: 10.1111/0033-3352.00137

[94] Smith and Sosin, *Op.Cit.*

[95] See; Coleman, 1990; Stinchcombe, 1968

[96] Stinchcombe, *Op. Cit.*

[97] Arthur Stinchcombe *Constructing Social Theory* (Chicago: University of Chicago, 1968).

[98] Dror, *Op. Cit.*

[99] See Samuel P. Huntington and Myron Weiner (eds). *Understanding Political Development,* New York: Addison-Wesley Educational Publishers, 1987. Also see Huntington, *Political Order in Changing Societies*, (New Haven: Yale University Press, 1968).

[100] Ezekiel 36:1, *Holy Bible*

[101] Olivia M. McDonald, *Analytical Bridge for the Literary Mind: A Unique Primer in Public Policy. Limited Access Document, Grace House Publishing. 2006*

NOTES FOR CHAPTER 8

[102] Hogwood and Gunn, *Op.Cit.*

[103] Dunn, *Op.Cit.*

[104] *Ibid*, p.60

[105] *Ibid*, p.59

[106] See: Christopher H. Achen, *The Statistical Analysis of Quasi-Experiments.* (Berkley: University of California Press, 1986); Also see: Adam Przeworski and Henry Teune *The Logic of Comparative Social Inquiry.* Malabar: Krieger Publishing Company, 1982).

[107] James Coleman, *Foundations of Social Theory* (Cambridge, MA: Harvard University Press, 1990).

[108] Dunn, *Op.Cit.*

[109] *Ibid.59*

[110] Brian Hogwood and Lewis A. Gunn, *Public Policy in the Real World (New York: Oxford University Press, 1984) Also See Brian Hogwood and B. Guy Peters, Policy Dynamics (New York: St. Martin Press, 1983)*

[111] *Ibid.*

CONCLUSION

[112] *Romans 12:21, New American Standard Bible*

[113] Willard, *Op. Cit.* 277.

[114] Bachrach, *Op. Cit.*

[115] *Webster Deluxe Unabridged Dictionary*(New York: Random House, 2005)

[116] See http://hotair.com/archives/2007/02/08/video-husham-al-husainy-on-hannity-colmes/

[117] Ezekiel 37:3, *Holy Bible*